#Walt

One Family's Desperate Attempt to Save Their Beloved Cat from Cancer

by

David I. Antokal

DORRANCE
PUBLISHING CO
EST. 1920
PITTSBURGH, PENNSYLVANIA 15238

Dorrance Publishing Co
585 Alpha Drive
Pittsburgh, PA 15238
Visit our website at www.dorrancebookstore.com

ISBN: 979-8-88812-238-9
eISBN: 979-8-88812-738-4

"There is a large mass in his ascending colon. I am very concerned that this might be cancer..."

And then my heart stopped. I went completely numb. I was in a gas station parking lot speaking with my mother when the call from the veterinarian came in.

The COVID-19 pandemic was still in full force during this time period. We had dropped our cat off at a specialty vet practice about an hour ago. The protocol was they come to your car, pick up your pet, then the vet would call you.

"Mom, let me call you back." I hung up with her and tried to breathe as I flipped back to the vet on the other line.

"I would like to take an ultrasound guided needle biopsy of this while he is still under anesthesia. This is very likely lymphoma or adenocarcinoma."

I asked about the prognosis for both.

"Two to six months for lymphoma, and with adenocarcinoma, it depends. It's aggressive but if you catch it early and remove all of it, it can be curative if it hasn't spread. "His frail condition is concerning, and I'm not sure he would make it through a surgery."

My heart sank deeper, as I knew Walter had been struggling with these symptoms for months. I called my mother back, and when I tried to speak, nothing came out. After a long pause, the only sound I could make was the sound of tears, and then, "They think he has cancer."

It was December 2020. We were all still in the midst of this depressing pandemic. I imagine many people were grateful to have family and their extended family; the beautiful creatures we call pets. Who is the real pet? Is it the innocent animal who shows unconditional love and provides companionship or the complicated and distracted human being who desperately craves said love and companionship? I understand animal adoption rates skyrocketed during the pandemic as people were forced to suspend everyday living and spent more time at home. Our home was always filled with love, both human and fur babies. Now, part of my family was in grave danger, and the news rocked us to the core.

How did we get here? In the summer of 2020, Walter was a regular patient in a local vet clinic that specialized in cats. His visit in July showed that he had lost more weight since his last year's visit. The vet suspected he had inflammatory bowel disease (IBD) and concurrent pancreatitis. She tested him for pancreatitis, which came back presumably positive, and promptly put him on prednisolone, which is a steroid that reduces inflammation and can increase appetite. I inquired about a dietary change in order to assist with weight gain.

At the height of his beastliness, Walter topped out at 13 pounds. He was a tall and muscular, short-haired domestic tuxedo cat with equal parts sappy lover boy and wild child. Walter now weighed 9.4 pounds. It had been a slow and progressive downward trend in his weight. Of note, he was now 15 years old; not exactly young for a cat.

Walter had always been an unusual cat. He was very affectionate, curious, and personal. However, he was definitely choosy about who he would let close to him. I can recall when we lived in Georgia, my strong-willed mother came to visit. Walter was rather wild and unruly when he was young, and my mother had disdain for his habits. These habits included jumping on tables, sitting on chairs, and basically doing whatever tickled his fancy. We were so smitten with him that we allowed him to do pretty much whatever he wanted. One evening, my mother sat on the bed where myself, my wife, and Walter were. She pointed a finger at Walter and began to lecture him about his behavior. I watched incredulously as Walter scrunched his face and let my mom know who the boss was by slapping her across the face with his paw. There was no scratch, as he didn't extend his claws, but the message was sent: "This is my house, and you're a guest in it." This became a laughing point for years to come.

We had been very attentive cat parents, and he always had an annual visit. He had his share of health issues over the years. He was about six months when we adopted him and promptly had a severe case of feline herpes virus days after adoption. He spent time in kitty ICU for several days and almost died. Thankfully, he made a full recovery from that episode.

The bonding between man and cat is accelerated when faced with the prospect of losing your beloved little buddy. Walter and I bonded early and strongly. At three years old, Walter began noticeably limping. This limp ended up being a torn ACL, which, of course, required reconstructive surgery. There was never any hesitation about that surgery, which relieved him of his limp and provided him years of improvement and pain relief. I recall one of the orthopedic surgeons I worked with lamenting, "Your cat's surgery costs more than I receive from insurance for the same surgery."

Over the years, he had ear mites, allergies, eye infections, and as he got older, he had chronic constipation. His chronic constipation required many vet visits and was a stubborn issue. On the medical high-maintenance scale, Walter scored a solid 10.

Walter also had definitely used up some of those nine lives you read about cats having. When we lived in Tulsa, OK, Walter decided to run out into the middle of a four-lane road in front of our house. We watched in horror as he dashed out and froze when the inevitable end-of-life car barreled towards him. We were yelling and halfway out into the street when the sympathetic driver hit the brakes and swerved, narrowly missing him. We yelled for him to come back, and for once, he actually listened. He streaked back towards us, and with our hearts in our throats, we gasped a sigh of relief that no other cars were coming. We put his outdoor activities on high security after this incident.

Apparently Tulsa was the perfect venue for Walter to act out. One random Tuesday night, I was woken up with my wife yelling in my face. I cannot repeat what she said but it went something like "'Your f*****g cat just pissed on my head!"

My wife had fallen asleep on the couch and, as she tells the story, woke up with a warm, stinging sensation on her forehead. She looked up just in time to see Walter's butt hovering over her sleepy head. My response to this made things worse, as I laughed uncontrollably. At the time, my wife was mad, but as time went on, she told the story and elicited more laughter than I ever could.

Truth is, most people probably would've opened the door and tossed Walter out. He was beautiful, lovable, and very entertaining. However, he also had an issue with inappropriate urination. Despite visits to several vets, including at least one behavioral vet, Walter kept pissing on objects outside the litter box. A shirt, bag, or any other item that hit the floor was usually urinated on in short order. If you left your shoes in a different place, you usually put your foot in a wet shoe.

Visitors were warned about this, and several left with Walter's mark on their stuff. One particular weekend, my parents came to visit. They were compliant with the Walter piss protocol and adhered to it. Right before they left, their luggage was at the front door, ready to be placed in the car. Here came Walter, and before I could beat him to the luggage, he unloaded. It was like clockwork. As a matter of fact, during our wedding weekend, he urinated on the air mattress my stepfather was sleeping on each day. It was almost like he was sending a message that stated: "It's time for you to go."

On the last night, the air mattress had no air as Walter had punctured it. I'll be damned if it didn't also have a fresh puddle of urine on it, too.

I can't imagine most people would've tolerated this behavior for a day, let alone well over a decade, but we did. He got Prozac transdermally in an attempt to stem this behavior, but it only helped slow down the piss train a little.

When Walter was in his early years, he was quite the acrobat. Taking a running start, he was easily able to jump onto a six-foot fence and perfectly balance on the top. It was incredible to watch him run with long strides like a greyhound. Fast was an understatement, as he was a blur when he ran. Walter's ACL tear and subsequent repair did not slow him down much. He maintained his athleticism and feline prowess.

When we lived in Georgia, I used to "walk the property" with him. We would take walks around our large yard, which bordered a running creek. Oftentimes, Walter would take off running after rabbits. One day, he came very close to catching a baby rabbit before I intervened and prevented an unnecessary slaughter. I was unable to prevent the day he snatched a bird mid-flight; I felt terrible when this happened. The bird flew away and hopefully survived his ordeal with our black and white ball of relentless energy.

Walter was hyper aggressive until about the age of five. Getting up at night or in the early morning was not without peril. Many nights, I would get out of bed to walk down the hallway and was greeted with a seething pain in my calf muscle. Walter would ambush me with that patented dual fang assault into my lower leg, which always made me release a loud yowl. There were times he would blow through his nose like a little bull, daring you to try to run past him to the safe confines of the bed. You had to tread carefully, as he would wait for you to make your move before he lunged to bite. Occasionally, I would get past him and would dive into the bed with Walter diving after me, hot on my trail. If this sounds insane, it most certainly was!'

We often thought Walter was possessed in those early years. In fact, we would often hear a crazy warbling and broken meow sound at the bottom of the stairs. When we walked to investigate, he would clam up and would be sitting at the bottom of the stairs, staring up. Mischief was Walter's middle name, and he earned his reputation as a wild child.

Walter seemed to have a particular taste for kids. In 2007, I ruptured my Achilles tendon playing football. At the ripe old age of 37, I should have known better than to attempt a late comeback tour but did it anyway. As I laid up recovering in an air-boot while bombed on Percocet to dull the pain, Walter remained at my side. One evening, we had our dear friends over for a visit. Our friends' daughter, who was about eight at the time, came upstairs to the loft where Walter and I were sharing a recliner chair, watching television. I warned her not to aggravate Walter, but she just couldn't help herself. I nodded off for a moment and woke up to loud crying. I looked across the room and my eyes found Walter on top of Kaitlyn, who was crying. I yelled at him to stop, and he galloped over to my recliner. Kaitlyn was shaken but without a scratch. I leaned over the railing and called to my wife, "Walter is trying to eat Kaitlyn!"

Looking back, we all laughed about this story every time it was retold. In subsequent years, Walter gave two more children black eyes with his patented paw slap. One of those was one of our friend's son at our housewarming party, and the other was my wife's nephew, who also ignored the "do not disturb the tiger" warnings.

As wild and aggressive as he was, Walter was equal parts mushy cat lover boy. He would cuddle up right into your face each night for an extended cuddle session. It seemed that he especially liked when your arm was around him, snuggling him close. His purring was like a runaway lawn mower on high speed. I always found this to be very comforting after a hard or stressful day. He would kiss and nip your chin until it was sore. Bedtime was always a treat, except for your wet chin, which had been bathed in cat kisses and love nips.

You could seldom be in a separate room from him, as he would follow you everywhere. If he didn't see you, he would cry until you communicated with him or he found you. Forget being on a couch by yourself. The moment Walter saw you, he was in your lap and doling out kisses. The bonding was very strong between Walter and I. When my fiancé moved in with us, Walter was most likely jealous and was standoffish to her for a while. He eventually warmed up to her and bonded very strongly with her as well. Simba, my wife's tiny female cat, had no such luck.

We spent days slowly introducing Walter to his new sister. He seemed more eager to be friends than she did. Hissing and swatting was a usual event in our burgeoning cat house. One day, we left them both out and came home to a frightening sight. Simba had a chunk missing from her head. Apparently, they had been in a scrap, and she was on the losing end of it. Off to the vet we went for treatment. Thankfully, that incident did not repeat itself.

In 2010, my wife expressed interest in adopting a dog. I knew this would be treacherous since we had one cat in the house who was convinced he was a full-grown tiger. We ended up adopting a Chihuahua puppy at the pound named Barney. He was full on adorable and hyper. Of course, while at the pound, we also discovered a beautiful and unusual kitten who was just begging for a new home as well. Mayfield was charcoal colored with silver stripes as an undercoat. He was gentle, sweet, and just had to be part of a dual adoption. We took both home and watched Mayfield and Barney play wrestle at every opportunity.

Barney was crated, and Mayfield was being slowly introduced to his new brother and sister. Barney's trips outside of the safe confines of his crate were treacherous for obvious reasons. We cringed when he approached Walter. Our suspicions and fears were validated when an audible "pop" could be heard across the room. I was a boxing fan, and apparently Walter was too because he had a deadly right hook with that paw.

Having a dog was not going to work in our house. The resident King of the Jungle was not going to stand for it. Barney's experience in our cat house lasted about 3 weeks. He spent time in the crate, had play time outside of it, got beaten up by Walter, then retreated to his crate. It wasn't fair to him. Luckily, our lovely neighbor was a huge dog fan and took Barney in. Barney loved his new home and was befriended by all her other dogs. In fact, Barney loved his new home so much that he decided to expand his family. In a few months Barney had knocked up or neighbor's 12-year-old Chihuahua. We were all speechless to say the least!

Mayfield fared better than Barney in our house. He spent a few weeks in isolation due to worms, ear mites, and overall kitten sickness, but he soon was turned loose. Unfortunately, it didn't take long before he was subjected to an initiation ceremony. One afternoon, I witnessed Mayfield walk over to Walter and heard the dreaded "pop" sound. Mayfield was wobbly from the blow, and when I intervened, I noticed his eye didn't look right. Off to the vet's office we went. Apparently, Walter had tore the conjunctival membrane in Mayfield's eye, which required a minor surgery to repair. As loving as Walter could be, he also was extremely territorial and fierce when he wanted to be. He definitely ruled with an iron paw.

As the years rolled on, we moved several times. Our cats were very much our kids, and we couldn't imagine being without them. Every day I came home to see Walter, it felt like unwrapping a wonderful and loving present on Christmas. In fact, I told my wife this on many an occasion. There is just no way to explain the different type of bond you form with a cat. Their love has to be earned; they do not give it to everyone.

We moved with these cats to three different states, and they lived in apartments and homes.

Walter definitely enjoyed our house in OK with a pool. He would lay by the water and hide in the plants surrounding the pool. We found out that Walter could swim one day when he braved the water. It was a "cat paddle" that was never repeated! Any time we would have a pool party, he would be highly social and would interact and amuse the guests.

When we put that house up for sale, I received a frantic phone call from our realtor. I had put Walter in a carry crate for the open house. Apparently, he pulled off a Houdini escape, pranced into the living room, and promptly left the house in the middle of the open house. I ran home and found him sunning himself by the pool. It was typical Walter; strong willed and full of personality. The memories are priceless.

As our cats (we had three) got older, we decided to find a clinic that specialized in the care of cats. Our thought process was that if you only see cats as patients, you must be really good at cats. This clinic was about 20 minutes away from where we lived, but we wanted the best for our three fur babies.

Walter had been losing weight at a slow, steady pace for the past two years. During his visit in July 2020, the vet voiced her concern about his weight loss and recommended a full battery of lab work. She suspected either pancreatitis, inflammatory bowel disease (IBD), or both concurrently. We were already reading about both of these as we awaited his lab results.

Walter's lab results unequivocally showed an elevation in his pancreas specific markers. The vet also believed he had IBD. The plan was to start him on prednisolone (a steroid) to see if we could reduce the inflammation. Apparently, both of these disease processes can be chronic and can be managed medically. Oddly, there was no recommendation for any dietary changes, so I inquired.

The consensus decision was made to incorporate a high calorie diet in order to increase his caloric intake and hopefully his weight. The vet suggested a mainstream brand and scoffed at the multitude of other options that exist in the cat nutrition marketplace as "lacking studies." We were off to the pet store to go food shopping.

There are literally aisles full of cat and dog food choices. I understood the vet's position concerning the multitude of options and took her advice. We chose the Purina Pro line as his new diet and set off to fatten him up. I had no idea if this was going to work, but couldn't help but wonder why I was the one who had to suggest the dietary guidance. Nonetheless, we were optimistic that we could change things up in order to produce a positive change.

The prednisolone was a challenge. The liquid was bitter and caused foaming in our poor cat's mouth whenever we gave it to him. I researched the idea of a compounding pharmacy and found one that was agreeable to compound his medicine. The pharmacist owned a cat and sympathized with our plight. He was kind and happy to help us. They compounded the steroid into a vanilla liquid, and Walter had no problem taking it.

The course of steroids was on a schedule. It was to be given every day for a period of time followed by a decreasing dose in order to establish a baseline and steady amount in his system. Some of the side effects were potential development of diabetes, increased risk of infection due to immunosuppression, and an increase in appetite. The last side effect would be a welcome event in Walter's case.

As July rolled into August, we were not seeing much of a response from Walter's treatment and subsequent dietary changes. His weight was slowly decreasing, and his energy level was following suit. We were concerned but very determined to stay the course. We decided to try different food choices in order to tempt him to eat more. He was now on Mirtazapine, which is an appetite stimulant. Thankfully, this could be given via the transdermal route, so we rubbed it in his ear, making sure to alternate ears every couple of days.

We frequently changed food choices, as the vet's food recommendation was not to Walter's liking. There is no telling how much time and money we spent buying up different brands, textures, and flavors in the various pet stores, both in person and online. We were in constant contact with this vet clinic's office, and they recommended no changes. This was turning out to be an expensive and time-consuming labor of love.

As we rolled into October, Walter continued to lose weight, energy, and his appetite. We were concerned that his downward progression required further intervention. I booked an appointment with his vet at the cat clinic. After she examined him, she informed me that he was still losing weight and that, "Walter is the equivalent of 80 years old in human years; he is an old cat."

I was shocked she would say that. Was this her way of saying we should pull the plug and throw up the white flag?

I pushed forward and asked what our options were. She volunteered that we could consider an abdominal ultrasound. Of course, they didn't offer that service at their clinic but had an internal medicine vet that visited and performed this service periodically. I was stunned that the cat clinic, which described itself as a full-service facility, did not offer this service. When she gave the the available dates and times for this service, I realized that it was very limited and didn't fit our work schedules. There had to be another way to do this.

During the drive home, I realized that this vet clinic appeared lazy, disinterested, and in my mind, they had no business touting their "specialty in cats." I imagined how this vet would feel if someone informed her that one of her family members was "80," so "it's time to let go."

I was now extremely motivated to pursue the internal medicine vet they recommended outside of the not-so-caring confines of the cat clinic. Walter deserved much better care, and so did we. The cat clinic was fired as far as we were concerned; it was time to move on. Hopefully, it was not too late.

It took me a while to locate and book an appointment with the internal medicine vet. We were in a COVID world where everyone was freaked out, and appointments were hard to come by. The practice was one of the larger ones in the area; kind of a one-stop shop, if you will. Their reputation was one of being able to handle anything in the pet world.

We were now into early December before the appointment was booked. It was the first available appointment we could find. My wife and I waited in our car for them to pick up Walter. We were still in the throes of COVID, and you weren't able to meet the vet in person. After dropping him off, we found a local diner for an anxious breakfast. During breakfast, I was able to speak with the vet about Walter's history and why we were bringing him to see an internal medicine vet. She sounded confident that she would be the one to finally figure out what was wrong with our rapidly deteriorating feline fur baby. We were about to find out otherwise.

After the conversation with Walter's internal medicine vet in the car, I gathered myself and then shared the horrific news with my wife. Unfortunately, she was at work, and the tears could readily be heard on the other line. We did not know what exactly was wrong, but when the "C" word is mentioned, it certainly sends a cold shiver down your spine. The thought of only having a few months hurt so bad that neither one of us wanted to discuss that possibility. We were now destined to wait for the diagnostic results and needed to show Walter that we loved him even more. Each day was an opportunity to shower him with affection and love. Walter's fur was wet for a few days as it attempted to soak up the tears of two heartbroken cat parents.

The waiting game was tough sledding. Not knowing when that phone call would come and where you might be was hard. Our appointment was on Thursday, and the call came in when I was at work on Tuesday.

"Non conclusive" was the word of the day. The pathology was inconclusive, which meant that they couldn't identify cancer but couldn't rule it out either. I was optimistic perhaps that he didn't have cancer. The vet still adamantly thought he had some type of cancer, perhaps a rarer kind like leiosarcoma or osteosarcoma. Given the lack of a definitive diagnosis, her suggestion was to start a months course of amoxicillin, the "hail Mary" as she described it. Her thought process was that there could be a small chance this was some type of granuloma from a chronic infection. Apparently, the best course of action was to surgically remove this section of colon to readily determine what this was. Of course, she also felt that Walter might not survive such a surgery.

The concrete plan was to reassess him and repeat the diagnostic work after one month of amoxicillin.

With a potential life risking surgery on the horizon, we already were working on a plan to optimize Walter's condition.

Much like the cat clinic vet, this vet also offered no nutritional counseling and offered nothing beyond what the diagnostic work revealed. Being that I worked in anesthesia, I know something about the benefit of optimizing a patient for surgery. In his current state, Walter was a poor surgical candidate. He was underweight, weak, and rather frail. I would say he was the patient who needed a tune-up prior to the stress of surgery. We needed to figure out a way to put weight on him and make him stronger in case surgery was in his immediate future. I decided to reach out to a holistic vet. After conducting a search online, I chose one who did house calls, as we didn't want to stress Walter out any further. I called the internal medicine vet to see if she would be okay to work alongside a holistic vet, and she was agreeable. I was in the process of assembling a team of vets on his behalf; Team Walter was being assembled.

My wife and I found that our stress level was pervading all areas of our life. There were many days we found ourselves crying at work in a bathroom, in the car, and at home. One of these days sticks out above the rest. After work one evening in late December, my wife and I were visiting with Walter on our bed. He looked so frail and sunken in. My wife was softly crying as we loved on him.

"I'm afraid that he is dying," she whispered. He looked gaunt and very thin, his fur matted and a yellowish tint.

"We are going to get him stronger," I reassured her. I was so determined to save this beautiful cat's life that my determination was fighting actively against my despair. Trust me, I cried a lot in private places but tried not to do it in front of my wife. I sure did cry a lot in Walter's fur as I held him close and pleaded with him to keep fighting. We were all in this together. Losing was not an option.

The holistic vet arrived in her own car, black scrubs, and with a large bag. She was an eccentric lady, very talkative and interesting. She was someone who started in Western veterinary practice and had branched out to incorporate Chinese herbal medicine, acupuncture, and a host of other modalities. Our interest was in nutritional counseling and herbal medicine. After spending about an hour chatting with us, she made her way into our bedroom to examine Walter in his own bed. Normally, Walter did not like to be examined by a stranger, but in his weakened state, he didn't seem to care. She felt that Walter had a blood flow issue; "cold blood stagnation" I believe was her Chinese medicine diagnosis. How real was this? We didn't know, but we were willing to try anything to help him. She prescribed him some herbal remedies "Eight Gentlemen" and "Wei Chi Booster." She also changed him to a higher calorie diet, recommended fish oil, and then surprised us. She pulled out acupuncture needles and asked permission. "Why not?" was our response. I'm shocked he tolerated it, but Walter was the recipient of about six needles in various parts of his body. Acupuncture is supposed to boost immune function, appetite, and overall wellbeing with cancer and other conditions. It looked bizarre, but we had nothing to lose.

Before she left, she emailed me her diagnosis and plan for Walter. Her email also contained copies of the reports from the internal medicine vet. These reports contained information that the internal medicine vet hadn't discussed with us, and we were shocked when we read them.

It dawned on me that Walter's thoracic and abdominal X-rays were never discussed with me. We were so caught up in what was going on in his colon that we had forgotten the other diagnostic tests. I suppose the assumption was that no news is good news. Apparently, this was not the case. In her report, the internal med vet and her radiologist both noted a suspicious area on Walter's manubrium. The manubrium in a cat is akin to the sternum in a human being. They noted concern that there could be an aggressive bone mass present. Wow, she never mentioned this to us, and we never received these reports. I called several times to the clinic, but it took two weeks before I received a return call. I told her that I was surprised she hadn't mentioned this.

"Well, the only way to be sure would be to repeat all of the studies and then make a determination."

A new level of anxiety was now born, and it was mixed with disappointment and anger. It got worse. Her reports indicated that his colonic mass was in the ascending colon. The radiologist who read the report noted a mass in the descending colon. Which was it? When asked, the answer I got was, "Well, it depends on how you look at the films."

Huh…? My level of trust and confidence in this vet were evaporating faster than the ounces that were falling off my poor cat. The level of disregard and oversight was astounding. I started to think that Walter's team of vets would be going through an addition by subtraction at some point in the near future. My wife, who was a nurse, was furious at the level of abstract confusion that had been presented to us.

I work alongside pathologists, radiologists, and a host of other medical specialists. I made a point to bring the pathology report and X-rays to work for a second opinion. Granted, a feline radiograph would be different than what they usually read, but it would be worth an opinion. The radiologist looked at the manubrium X-ray and said, "There is no sign of a mass or tumor on this film." He also felt the film quality was somewhat poor. This was a relief.

Next stop was pathology. The pathologist was kind enough to read the report and shrugged when he said, "It appears they probably did not aspirate enough cellular material to identify what this is. If it were cancer, you would at least see enough to know."

It seems that the vet had not aspirated an adequate amount of cellular material, thus it was impossible to glean an adequate diagnosis. Thus far, we had no diagnosis for the colon, a potential misdiagnosis based on the thoracic film, and a questionable location of where this mass was in his colon. I paid over $1,800 for this visit and had no answers. Worse yet, we were wasting time, as cancer is quite the time-dependent disease. The longer it's undiagnosed, the more time it has to metastasize.

The good news, if there was any, was that Walter was beginning to gain weight. He had dropped down to a gaunt 8.2 pounds and now was about a half a pound heavier. His appetite was better, and his activity level was a tad better. While as before most of his time was spent in bed, now he was coming downstairs to socialize a little more. We were very optimistic about this.

Unfortunately, his bowl habits were still concerning. Some days, there was a little blood in his stool; other days, the stool was too dark for our liking. There also were many days where the stool was very loose. It was obvious that he had issues that needed to be diagnosed. We were now getting close to the one-month mark on amoxicillin, and his condition was marginally better. We needed answers quickly.

In mid-January, I received a call from the internal medicine vet. She suggested it was now time to reexamine Walter and repeat all the diagnostic work we had done. To be fair, this was unfair. We had just wasted a month, and now we were supposed to start all over again. She also recommended a "needle guided bone biopsy of the manubrium"." I listened and took it all in as she spoke, knowing that neither my wife or I could trust her moving forward. After she spoke, I simply asked, "When would you be available to do this?"

Her answer floored me.

"I'll be available in about a month."

Someone pinch me because I must've been dreaming this. I was speechless and just said, "Okay."

I hung up and called my wife, who responded in a fashion that cannot be reproduced using non-vulgar words. Knowing that Walter would probably be dead by the time this vet obtained a legitimate diagnosis and plan, we decided it was time to fire her and move on.

Time was now truly of the essence, so it needed to be done quickly. I worked with an RN who had suggested a different large practice in town that handled complex cases. I decided to call them in order to beg for a quick appointment with their internal medicine vet. In the back of my mind, I also knew that I would be revisiting the poor experience we had with this now terminated vet and her multi-specialty group. I was determined to prevent this from happening to someone else's pet. However, I didn't have the energy or the time to fully deal with it; I had a life to save. I was able to get a quick appointment, and we were about to add yet another vet to Walter's growing stable.

We got a quick appointment with an internal medicine vet, and we were on our way again. This time around, we knew there was a good chance that he might be diagnosed with cancer, which made things mentally easier, as we were prepared for anything. The COVID protocol for drop off was the same, and the visit was uneventful. The vet was able to get a good sample for pathology, and she also felt that this was highly suspicious for cancer. The visit was on a Thursday, and on Monday, the phone call came in.

"Adenocarcinoma of the descending colon," was the clear diagnosis. The awful news was provided by an unfamiliar voice. It was a male vet; more specifically, a male vet intern. This bothered me, as I was expecting the female we had originally spoke with. This vet intern made it rather clear that he didn't feel Walter was a surgical candidate.

"There is not much we can do, as it appears to be advanced cancer."

I asked him if chemo was an option, and he felt that it wasn't. I felt a cold sweat running down my back, and a sense of hopelessness was creeping in like a poisonous fog.

"Please have the regular vet call me ASAP," I said as my mind was still reeling from this seemingly hopeless news. I was already preparing a plan B, which was going to consist of any type of alternative treatment we could find and perhaps yet another opinion.

To my surprise, the regular internal med vet returned my call quickly. She also had a different spin on current events.

"I spoke to surgery, and they told me that if this was a canine, then he would not be a good candidate. Feline has a much better prognosis for surgical intervention."

I felt like an elephant was lifted off my chest. As I called my wife, I was still annoyed about the miscommunication but very grateful that there was at least hope; any hope was good at this point.

We immediately requested a surgical consult, and unfortunately, it was not available for several weeks. In a bit of insanity, I actually reached out to the former vet practice to see if they had anything sooner. Thankfully, they didn't, and I made a point to plead my case to his current vet.""

"Please get him in; we have already lost months trying to get a diagnosis, and we really want to save him," was the gist of what I said. To my happy surprise, this worked, and they booked him a surgical consult one week out.

We had a new concern moving forward. Walter was quite anemic according to his new lab results. It appeared to be either from chronic inflammation and/or the tumor bleeding. After his internal med consult, it was determined that he would need a blood transfusion prior to surgery which carried its own risks of transfusion reaction. I deal with this type of thing frequently in my line of work, so I understood. He was a high-risk surgical candidate, and we knew that there was a good chance he might go into surgery the same day of his surgical consult. This meant that when we dropped Walter off for this appointment, the possibility existed that it might be the last time we saw him alive. The thought of this was overwhelming, and there were many tears shed during the lead up to this appointment.

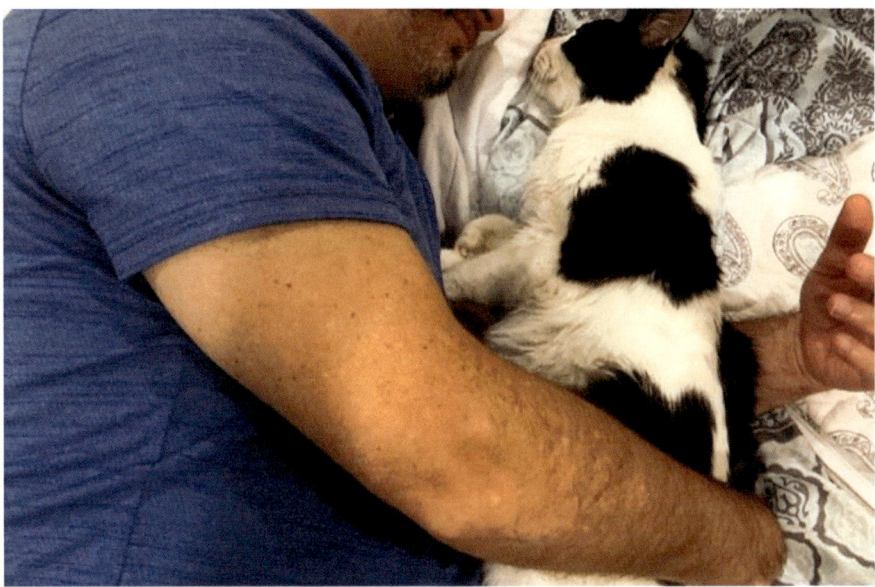

Every day, we loved on him as much as we could. Cats have very large eyes for their size, and looking into Walter's eyes, I feel like he understood that we were trying to save him. I actually knew he loved us as much as we loved him and didn't want to leave us. He was a very tough little fella, and he would need every bit of this "cattitude" moving forward. We were at the crossroads and knew that this was the only chance he had at survival. We would not stand by and allow cancer to take him. The decision had already been made: We were going to fight this cancer with everything we had, and it meant taking risks. If we did nothing, Walter would die a slow, miserable death. Surgery gave him a fighting chance to recover and live out his senior years. Our family was in a fight against a formidable enemy. The cancer needed to go.

How do you decide as a pet owner when the right time is to euthanize your pet? This is a sensitive, somewhat delicate issue, and there is much debate. There are lots of opinions on this subject, and the reading list is lengthy. Our opinion is one of quality of life and coexisting medical conditions. In Walter's case, his quality of life pre-cancer was great. He also had no other acute medical issues. The thought process was that if this tumor could be removed, perhaps it could be curative. Worst case scenario was that he didn't make it through surgery and passed over the rainbow bridge while he was sleeping.

Somewhere in between was where we figured he would land. That scenario would involve his quality of life going way up post-tumor removal, and then we'd figure the rest out post surgery. With this in mind, we were off to see the surgeon.

In the month leading up to this point, we had Walter on medicinal mushroom powders. He was receiving two different brands, and they covered the vast gamut of mushrooms studied for cancer fighting benefit. Maitake, shiitake, lions mane, turkey tail, chaga, etc. They were all present, and we were sneaking these into his food twice a day. It was definitely a challenge, and oftentimes, we had to use baby food as a medium to deliver the hidden cargo. I was also giving him coenzyme Q10, which is a potent antioxidant. We had been reading a lot online and in pet owner forums, which provided a lot of information. We added fish oil for the anti-inflammatory effects and the Chinese herbal medicine recommended by our holistic vet.

We were doing all we could to make him stronger and to keep his cancer from spreading as much as we could. It was certainly a full time job. It is sometimes said that dogs spend their lives as loyal servants, but cats consider people their servants. There might be some truth to this, as we were attending to his every need. In Walter's case, his servants were fighting very hard to save the Lion King.

I also had started researching other modalities of treatment online. IP6 is an antioxidant otherwise known as inositol hexaphosphate that apparently has some efficacy against cancer. Arteminisin is yet another one. Some people used turmeric or circumin as a potent anti-inflammatory. CBD oil used alone or in conjunction with THC, which is the active component of marijuana, is also used by many who are treating dogs and cats with cancer. I read about people using low-dose naltrexone, a protocol using Tagamet and Benadryl for some types of cancer, and licorice root. There was much to read about, but all of it begged a question. How much in the way of sound clinical research was actually supporting these alternative treatments?

The counter argument was also interesting. There are many people who believe that big Pharma works against alternative treatments that show promise if they cannot profit from them. I would certainly hope that isn't true, but some people make a compelling case for this theory. There was a lot of research and a lot to think about.

We showed up for the surgical consult at 10:00 AM with a hungry cat who had been fasted after midnight. My wife and I were both there in the parking lot; we knew inherently that Walter would be going in for surgery today. There were many tears shed, and we both took turns holding him. Previous drop offs usually involved Walter looking back at me in his crate when the exchange took place. This was a different day. When I gave the vet tech the crate, Walter didn't look back at us. I almost felt like he knew and there was something of a steely resolve in all of us to get this event moving full steam ahead. This was his only chance at survival.

With tears in our eyes, we watched Walter being carried into the facility.

It didn't take long for the surgeon to call me.

"We are planning to do surgery for him today. He will need the blood transfusion first, as he is anemic. I will do my best to get all of this cancerous colon out of him. The procedure has risks of dehiscence, infection, and recurrence of the cancer."

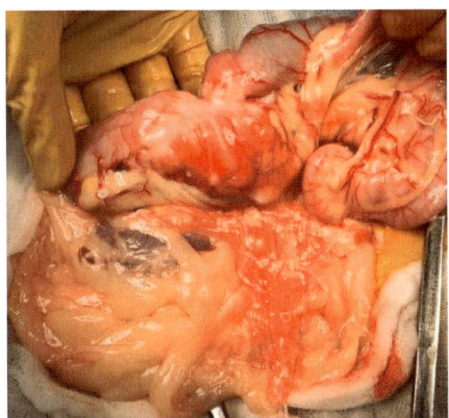

We were aware of the risks and were committed to setting up a solid kitty ICU at home for what came after. Walter was going to have an Ileo-colic colectomy with reanastamosis. In layman's terms, this meant that the junction of his ileum and large intestine were going to be removed and reconnected. He had battled constipation for years, and it was obvious that this might have been a contributing factor to his cancer development. Apparently, cancer thrives in an inflammatory state, and it had been festering in Walter undetected probably since at least last summer. We were on pins and needles after the drop off. This was going to be one long, anxious day.

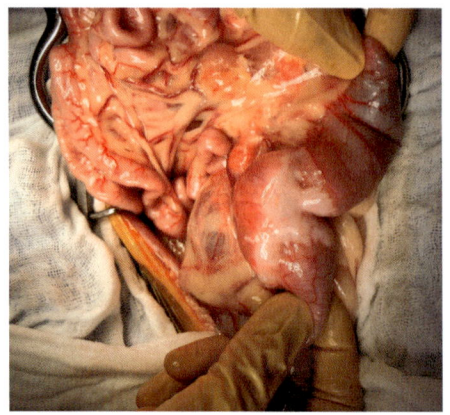

The waiting game is difficult, to say the least. Mentally, you don't want too quick of a phone call, nor do you want not to hear anything at all. I suppose the mental gymnastics we play in our head are typically far worse than anything we encounter in real life. In our case, I couldn't wait and called for an update several hours later. He had done fine getting his blood transfusion, which was hurdle number one. The surgery hadn't even started yet. Wow, we had a long way to go! Several hours later, at around 6:00 PM, I called again and spoke to the vet tech who did the anesthesia. She informed me that Walter was doing great! Snoopy dances for everyone! Apparently he had experienced a profound bradycardia (drop in heart rate) when the procedure started, which required her to intervene quickly. From there, everything seemed to go according to plan. She stated that Walter was awake, being treated for pain, and was looking good. We were in a state of relief and finally could exhale. One small step forward for Team Walter!

The surgeon followed up with her call. She told us that Walter had done well and that the tumor was larger than she thought. She felt that the cancer had definitely spread, as his local lymph nodes appeared to be destroyed by cancerous spread and were sent to pathology, and there were some spots in his omentum that were also suspicious for cancer. Our enthusiasm waned a bit on hearing this update. However, we were grateful for his making it through surgery and needed to wait for the full pathology report to truly know what the extent of his prognosis would be. We followed up a few hours later and were told that he was doing great and was actually already eating. This was surprising, and we turned into bed hoping the phone wouldn't ring during the night. The old adage "no news is good news" definitely applied here.

Thankfully, I woke up with no interruptions during the night and no missed calls or texts. I called the clinic and was told that Walter was doing so well that they were considering sending him home a day early! This felt like hitting the lottery to us. We were so excited to see him.

We arrived at the clinic early and waited in the parking lot. We decided to not contain our excitement anymore and started chanting "Free Walti" to entertain ourselves. About 30 minutes later, out came a vet tech carrying the familiar blue crate, and there was Walter...

He was alert and meowing when he saw us. Tears of joy cascaded as we were reunited. Walter was alive, doing well, and going home!

In anticipation of Walter's triumphant return home, we had created a cat ICU in our office. We had purchased a large dog crate, inflatable collar to prevent licking of his wound, pads, etc. The goal was now to limit post surgical movement, especially any type of jumping or running. Knowing Walter, this was going to be very difficult. It did not take long before he was crying to escape his new confinement. My wife and I spent much of our time at home medicating him for pain, feeding him, changing pads, etc. It was definitely a full time job after we came home from our full time jobs. The crying and whimpering caused my wife to spend many nights in the office, where she slept with Walter on the couch. We had a ramp, which we encouraged him to use instead of jumping, but you had to watch him carefully. Jumping could cause the wound to dehisce,which would be a surgical emergency. We had come too far for this to happen.

While his appetite was good, he spent a lot of time straining to defecate, which was concerning. I had to call the vet several times to confirm what we were seeing was normal post operative recovery. As it turns out, the type of cancer and surgery that he had was relatively rare in cats. As usual, Walter had to be a pioneer; it was in his nature.

He was so happy when we came in to visit with him. He would purr like a motor boat and would seek out cuddle time.

We had to make it out of the seven to 10 day mark to get out of the woods for complications to his healing surgical site. We were going to make it happen no matter what.

We forged through the first 10 days and were now onto the next phase. We released the beast into the rest of our home and couldn't be happier. The happiest time for all of us was having our cuddle buddy back in the bed. The bedtime cuddles were epic. When I laid down to sleep, Walter was already waiting for me. I'd get under the covers, and he would follow, making sure that my arm was around him before he'd purr himself to sleep. My wife would then cuddle in on the other side. It was delightful and very comforting, especially knowing he had certainly burned another of his nine lives by surviving a treacherous surgery.

Walter gradually put weight back on and hit nine pounds, which was amazing. He had almost a 12 percent weight gain since his lowest back in December. The energy level was also impressive as he wrestled with his cat brother Mayfield and chased his sister Simba around the house. Dinner time brought out his patented "Tiger Trot," where he would prance around the house in a slow trot with his tail up to get his feast on. It was like old times.

Next stop was the chemotherapy consult, but we also had additional plans to fight this cancer. We were planning to throw the kitchen sink at his cancer, and defeat was not going to be an option.

Two weeks after surgery, Walter was healing great and had more energy than he'd had in a long time. I'd refer to this as his second "kittenhood," as he appeared younger. His appetite was great, and he'd already put on almost a pound post operative. He was almost 9.6 pounds, which was roughly an 18 percent increase in his body mass.

We started to take very long walks on the seawall behind our home. The neighbors were stunned when they saw a cat leading a couple on the daily stroll. One day sticks out in particular. While walking close to one of the docks, I heard a loud splash. Walter and I turned around and there were two manatees looking at us. Walter went out on the dock for a closer look. I'm sure a cat born in GA had never seen such a thing, and it was hilarious to see. There were other walks where dolphins made an appearance as well. These walks were great for all of us, and we could take a deep breath and just enjoy living in the moment.

My wife and I had a routine for Walter that occurred each late afternoon. We called it the "love sandwich." When we both came home from work, we would go out into our courtyard and sit on the couch. Walter would inevitably find us quickly and jump on up for cuddles. We would take turns holding, cuddling, and kissing him. The purrs, drools, and contentment were priceless.

This practice would be repeated in the bed each night before settling in. We'd lay on each side of Walter and smother him with love and affection. He returned the affection in kind. It was a special kind of love fest that we shared with him and made all of us grateful to be in the moment.

Unfortunately, the pathology report confirmed the worst. Walter had an aggressive adenocarcinoma that had already infiltrated his lymph nodes and had spread into his omentum. His official prognosis was two months. This was an absolutely horrifying prospect. The thought of this vile cancer taking the scenic route in a tour around our beloved cat's body was nauseating, and the tears flowed readily. I thought of all the wasted time from his initial visit in early July until his surgery in early February.

There was a grotesque amount of time wasted that allowed this cancer to take root and spread. I had to contain the anger I felt at what I could only perceive as some really below-the-line veterinary care he had received at the cat clinic and then the multi-specialty clinic as well. In my opinion, this was most certainly a case of blatant malpractice, but this would have to wait. Our priority at the moment was gearing up in a fight to the death against this malignant and metastatic monster that had taken root in our fur baby.

We were getting close to our chemotherapy consult, and I had been in touch with a company named Torigen. I had been doing a lot of online research in my bid to give Walter the best chance to beat his cancer. Torigen had created a novel autologous vaccine to help cats, dogs, and horses battle cancer. I actually spoke to the CEO of Torigen, and she thought he would be a good candidate to receive the vaccine. She was an impressive woman to say the least and I had a lot of respect for what she and her company were doing.

The process was interesting, to say the least. When your pet had surgery to remove a mass, it was to be saved and frozen, but not with formalin (preservative). This mass would then be sent by the vet clinic to Torigen via overnight mail, frozen in a box with dry ice. The mass would then be dissected, the cancer cells deactivated, and then a vaccine would be created with the specific cancer cells that your pet has. The vaccine would be given once a week for three weeks with the hope that the pet's immune system would be able to mount an immune response to kill the cancer cells. We were so excited for this and also were hopeful that if it worked, perhaps other animals could benefit from Walter's participation. There were apparently less than 100 cats who had received this vaccine. There was about to be one more added to the list. Walter's surgically removed tumor was sent to Torigen, and a vaccine had been prepared.

I met the oncologist in the parking lot. He was a slender, middle-aged man who was well dressed and spoke very intelligently. We spoke about Walter's type of cancer and what the options were. He wasn't sure how responsive Walter's adenocarcinoma would be to either Doxorubicin or Cisplatin but said it would be worth a try. We decided to start with Cisplatin, and he offered it on the spot. I was hopeful we would start that day and proceeded with the plan. We also planned to give the first cancer vaccine the following day. It would have to be given once a week for three weeks.

I was still sick to my stomach about what was happening to my beloved little friend, but now the fear and angst had started morphing into something else. I had developed a steely resolve to fight for Walter's life with everything I could possibly offer him. Financially, we were fortunate, as I really had the means and didn't give a shit about how much any of this was going to cost. We were going to fight to the end, and it meant money, stress, and risks. In my mind, we were going to be "Walter Strong" in support of our brave fur baby.

His first chemo visit was uneventful, and he was sent home with nausea medicine. My resolve was so strong that I shed tears as I blared music on the way home. We were on to the cancer vaccine, and I never felt more determined to kick his cancer's ass. We were in this together, and I was going to go all in with Walter. Defeat was not an option.

We were throwing the kitchen sink at this cancer but also decided to not include everything at our disposal. The interesting thing about alternative treatments is how to know what the compatibility of different agents are. Are medicinal mushrooms compatible with an autologous cancer vaccine? Does any of this interact with chemotherapy? Do they work together or oppose each other as it relates to the immune system? How does IP6 factor in here? How does coenzyme Q10 fit in? Predictably, the oncologist offered no answers, as he couldn't possibly know. No amount of online research would provide answers. This was going to be best guess and judgement. In my opinion, the best guess was to not "muddy the picture." By this, I mean, too much was not going to be good. We decided to discontinue the mushroom powders, only give the COQ10 close to his doxorubicin doses (I had read that it protects the heart muscle from chemo damage), and would reassess as we went along. In my mind, I would keep the IP6 available as a backup plan for now. The alternative modalities begged the question of how much do you incorporate all at once? Does one treatment work with or against others? How do they interact? Will there be side effects? Will any of these treatments do more harm than good? There were no accessible studies and no clear answers. It was going to be a judgement call, and you could second guess until the cows came home.

The first Torigen vaccine was an uneventful process. I dropped him off at the clinic, and about 30 minutes later, they returned him to me in his crate. He didn't look any worse for wear. The odd thing about this is that Torigen suggests that there be an "observation period of a few hours" after the vaccine to assess for potential reaction. The oncologist obviously wasn't too concerned about this. In fact, he seemed rather skeptical about these types of treatments. He had explained to me that he had seen similar treatments before and, in some cases, saw a poor result when combining a vaccine with chemo.

We had nothing to lose in my opinion, given Walter's prognosis. He was certainly doing well at home. His weight was stable at around 9.5 pounds, his activity level was great, and things were looking up.

Doxorubicin was next up on the chemo train. In humans, doxy can be hard on cardiac tissue and has a dose dependent effect. I hadn't read this about cats but wondered if it applied. The oncologist stated it didn't, but I decided to stick with our plan in giving COQ10. One thing about Doxorubicin was unique and quite scary. If it leaked into the tissue via an infiltrated intravenous access, it could cause irreversible tissue damage. I read some horror stories online about this very thing. Thankfully, his second chemo dose was uneventful, and he then took his second vaccine the day after. Things were going well, and we were hopeful.

A few weeks went by, and it was Cisplatin time again. This was a quicker and easier process. Walter's weight and activity were both very stable. We were now taking long walks along the seawall behind our condo. I just couldn't get over the looks we got as Walter led us on his little safari trips. I realized when talking to people just how many animal lovers there were out there. People shared all kinds of stories about their pets and how much they meant to them. We certainly could relate, and this became a daily evening event we looked forward to. We also were able to have a nice balance between work, socializing, and taking care of our little fur baby. He was doing great.

With Walter doing well, I finally had time to address something I vowed to follow up on. I wrote a letter to the initial internal medicine vet's practice to share our feelings about the experience we had. The crux of the letter was one of "wasted time." Furthermore, the lack of urgency that the internal medicine vet showed was very distressing. I sent the letter certified mail and remarkably got a phone response from the owner of the company several days later. He apologized profusely and stated he would counsel the vet in question for her negligence and lack of acting in a timely fashion. He insisted that he wanted to refund our funds and did so via check. In this case, the money was irrelevant, as it could never replace the wasted time or bad feelings. However, the accountability was impressive and gave me hope that there could be positive change at that practice. The letter I sent to them is listed below.

February 20, 2021

Hi,

I'm writing this letter to share a sad and unfortunate experience my wife and I had with your practice. We have used ***** for all three of our cats. One of our cats Walter, had been referred to ***** by ***** for IBD which was not resolving. ***** felt that Walter needed an abdominal ultrasound and they apparently do not offer that service at *****.

On December 11, 2020, we had an appointment at your practice with *****. She performed an abdominal ultrasound and stated that there was a mass in Walter's ASCENDING colon. She recommended an ultrasound guided needle loc biopsy. She was concerned that the mass was either Lymphoma or Adenocarinoma but could be something else as well. We were told to await the biopsy results.

About 5 days later ***** called me to inform that the biopsy result was "inconclusive". She explained that lymphoma and adenocarcinoma were "very exfoliative" and that the results were "not exfoliative". If you review the results of the pathology report, the results did not reveal very much at all. ***** stated that she suspected a cancer, perhaps one of the other types such as a "leiomyosarcoma" or a "mast cell tumor". She also felt perhaps it could be a granulatoma from an infectious process, but less likely. Her recommendation was to start him on antibiotics "the hail Mary" as she described it, and to recheck in one month. She explained that the definitive diagnosis could only be made with surgery as more accurate samples could be obtained that way. She felt Walter was a risky proposition for surgery due to his age and frail status.

At this time, we decided to consult also with a holistic vet to gain some advice about dietary modifications, alternative treatments such as Chinese herbal medicine, omega 3's, etc. in case he did have some type of cancer. With her assistance, Walter was able to gain a pound during this time period. It is also during this time that I realized that ***** had never discussed with me the results of Walter's abdominal and thoracic x-rays. Reading *****'s full report that was sent to our holistic vet, it appeared that she was concerned about a potential "bone mass on his manubrium". I was surprised that this was not directly discussed with me. Also odd was the radiologist that read the report noted a mass in the "DESCENDING" colon. There appeared to be a contradictory report on the location of the mass.

I called to speak with ***** during the holiday season. I left a message with one of your staff members. I did not get a call back until several weeks later. When I did speak to***** she informed me that she was concerned about the manubrium having a potential lesion and stated the location of the colonic tumor was ASCENDING colon and that reading the film could be misleading.
OK.

In mid January I received a call from ***** advising that it was now a good idea to repeat Walter's diagnostic tests. She also thought it would be a good idea to explore "an ultrasound guided needle loc biopsy of the manubrium". When I asked ***** when she would be available to repeat the diagnostic tests the answer I got was stunning. "IN A MONTH". My wife and I decided to switch internal medicine doctors after this conversation and made an appointment with *****.

Three days after seeing Walter, his internal medicine vet at ***** diagnosed Walter with ADENOCARCINOMA of the DESCENDING colon. The pathology report was detailed and thorough. A surgery consult was advised but initially not immediately available. We realized now that Walter's only chance was to have immediate surgery. To this end, I reached back out to your practice to see if a surgical consult was available sooner. I got a call back from ***** who informed me that ***** was not available until Feb 15th and offered me a televisit with oncology or ***** if interested. I received a call from ***** shortly after this message and they quickly shuffled their schedule to squeeze Walter in.

On February 4th, Walter had his surgery consult and was taken into surgery the same day. He did well and was discharged the next day. They did a colectomy with anastamosis and sent biopsies of his regional lymph node and omentum. Unfortunately, the pathology report came back with metastasis in both samples. He just completed his first dose of chemotherapy, is enrolled with a company to receive an immunotherapy cancer vaccine, and is also receiving holistic integrative care.

Sadly, the initial prognosis we received was 2 months.

We saw ***** on December 11th. By our account, we wasted at least one month as ***** missed Walter's diagnosis. Had we waited for Walter's "recheck" with *****, we would have wasted an additional month (assuming ***** would have been able to successfully perform the ultrasound guided biopsy the second time in order to make a correct diagnosis). The x-rays performed at ***** <u>did not </u>show any lesion in the manubrium. **Sadly, ***** dropped the ball on Walter's diagnosis. More distressing is that we wasted time. The earlier this is diagnosed, the less chance the cancer has to spread. I'm pretty sure Walter would not be alive today if we had followed *****'s timeline of recommended treatment. It's almost miraculous Walter is alive today and actually hanging in there as we attempt to provide him with the very best treatment available.**

In summary, it's not bad enough that his diagnosis was missed; we wasted precious time. I also wasted over $1800 at your practice. In my opinion, that expenditure purchased me a missed diagnosis and too much wasted time. I think you should refund my money as it could be used in an attempt to prolong Walter's life. <u>I normally would not be writing this type of letter but if this were a human being, in my opinion this would border on medical malpractice</u>. I'm not eager to share bad reviews of your practice but it's easy to read just how disappointed we are with our experience at ***** I'm willing to discuss this further and to provide medical records upon request.

Sadly,

David Antokal

The following visit to the oncologist was bizarre, to say the least. I dropped Walter off early and didn't hear anything for several hours. I called in to check and was told that they were running behind. I finally got the call to come get him and was not greeted by the normal vet tech. The oncologist carried Walter out and said, "He couldn't get his chemo today. We were unable to get an adequate IV."

I felt terrible knowing Walter had spent a full day being poked and prodded to no avail. He also was sent home with a blood-soaked ear, which I discovered once I arrived home. I called the clinic and spoke to the vet tech who informed me that, "I'm so sorry. It must have happened in the scrum when he was fighting against us." Wow. I know he was a sassy cat with attitude, but a "scrum"?

My wife and I were pissed. Did they think we just wouldn't notice that our cat had a chunk missing from his ear? The disappointment with this visit was unfortunately a foreshadowing of his next appointment.

"Walter has a small mass under his incision line. It is small, seems to be subcutaneous, and attached to his abdominal wall."

I felt a cold sweat running down my back.

"Does this mean the chemo is no longer working?" I asked.

"It definitely means the Cisplatin is no longer working. We will proceed with the Doxorubicin and will recheck him in two weeks to see if the tumor shrinks."

He was able to get a needle biopsy of the mass just to confirm what we all painfully knew. His cancer had somehow been seeded into the area below his incision line. I knew from my line of work that surgery involving cancer had to be very carefully carried out to prevent spread of the diseased tissue. In this case, the oncologist thought it was either "seeded" or was just cancer being cancer. Adenocarcinoma was aggressive, and we knew it was a formidable enemy. Walter got his chemo, and I took him home, tears running down my face.

Once home, I decided to let Walter take his daily walk on the seawall. Despite this new tumor, his energy level was still good. He was walking along the seawall at a rapid pace and got too far ahead of me. In my quest to prevent Walter from going too far, I attempted to go around him in order to get in front and redirect him. I'd done this many times before, and it was always easy. Perhaps Walter was spooked at the bad news or just wasn't feeling himself because he spun himself around too quickly. And then his back leg slipped off...

...and then he fell off the sea wall into the murky water below. It was about a six-foot drop during low tide. It all seemed to occur in slow motion. I yelled out his name as I watched him hit the water below and submerge. I was mortified. I also was on my way into the water in a frantic bid to rescue him. He surfaced and began to doggy paddle when I grabbed him and held him out of the water. I reached up...and couldn't reach the top of the sea wall.

Instinctually, I put him above my head and shot him over the sea wall like a basketball player going for a three-point shot. Thankfully, he was on dry land. Now, what about me? I couldn't get out by reaching anything in particular and was only thinking about getting out to check on Walter. Did he aspirate the sea water? Was he okay? I dug my fingers on the top of that seawall and began the process of pulling my 175 pound, soaking wet body up by my fingertips. I could feel the barnacles cutting me was I strained to pull myself up. *I've got to get to Walter,* I thought.

Finally, I hoisted myself to the top.

Once I stood up, I locked eyes with Walter. He was soaked with his pupils fully dilated. He looked like he just saw a sea monster emerge from the depths of the ocean. Not a stupid cat, Walter took one look at me, turned around, and took off running. "

I saved your life now you're going to get yourself killed by a car! was my first thought. I had called to my wife, who was now also in full pursuit of a runaway Walter. She saw me on my knees soaking wet and had guessed what had happened.

Thankfully, there were no cars on our quiet street, and I finally caught up with Walter. He looked terrified and was breathing super fast. We figured he was in shock. We carried him home and dried him off, making sure to use some fresh cool water in order to get the salt water off his coat as best we could. I'm quite sure he was thinking, *That was probably the last sea wall walk I'll ever take...*

This was not a good day for Team Walter Strong.

It's amazing how a sick family member can bring a family closer together. The image of him falling into the water below was stuck in my mind on loop. It was traumatic for all of us and was also a tad comical at the same time. Re-telling the story drew both gasps and laughter from those we shared it with. Literally days later, we saw a five-foot bull shark trolling the waters of our canal. This added to the terror. I would've gone in after him if there was a shark, alligator, and sea monster waiting with an open mouth. It was just like that for us. We were all in this together.

The sea monster with the open mouth came in the form of a report from our oncologist after the latest visit at the oncology clinic. Walter's cancerous tumor had grown a bit after his Doxorubicin dose. This meant that chemo-therapy had failed. We were devastated all over again. This was a double-edged sword. On the one hand, I was deeply disappointed about the chemo failure. On the other hand, I was whole heartedly relieved that he no longer had to go through this torturous process of routine chemo visits. I had been told previously by one of the vet techs that, "Walter doesn't like it here." This made me feel really bad as the thought of him scared and suffering at the vet office was mortifying. There is certainly guilt associated with subjecting your pet to treatment they might not understand the need for.

The oncologist said we could try Palladia. Palladia is a chemo type of drug usually used in dogs but off label for cats. It is an oral agent that comes in pill form, and you have to handle it carefully. Palladia is supposed to disrupt the growth and spread of cancer cells and the blood supply to cancerous tumors. They gave him his first dose while in the clinic, and I knew we would have to have this compounded into a liquid somehow. Walter was very difficult to ad-minister pills to. We were on to the next treatment cycle.

The Palladia was compounded into a thick, yellow liquid that resembled a curry. I was very skeptical that he would take this without a fight. Boy, was

I right. The first attempt left him gagging, drooling, spitting, and with a stained yellow mouth. The loss of appetite was profound within a few days. This $200 yellow liquid was difficult to administer and left him also more lethargic than usual. Calls to the oncologist were unreturned, which was disappointing. Finally, we were told to bring him back for another visit. The oncologist examined him and then came out to speak with me.

"I don't think the Palladia is working for him." I had read that Palladia could take six weeks to work and passed that along to the oncologist. "Usually, we see results within about a week." Walter had taken four doses.

I asked what else we could do.

"Nothing," he replied. "I don't have anything else to offer."

Oh my God, we were being fired by the oncologist. He had put up the white flag and was waving it out in the parking lot.

"Do you have any holistic vets that you can recommend?" I asked.

He thought for a moment and then gave me the name of a vet practice that was about 30 minutes north of us. This was profoundly disappointing, as we were now on our own and had to put together a new plan of attack. The cancer was currently kicking our ass, and we had to fight back stronger.

The interesting part of being fired from oncology was that Walter no longer had a vet. He really didn't have a primary vet during chemo treatment either. His reports were being sent to the holistic vet we used a few times for acupuncture. She was helpful pre-surgery, but there was little to no communication after that. By my count, he had a team of five vets that had been whittled down to zero. Break up the Beatles! He needed a primary vet, and we decided to also contact the holistic vet referred by the oncologist.

On my way to work, every day, I passed a new pet hospital. I worked with a podiatrist who was raving during lunch one day about how good this new practice was. I decided to stop by on the way home from work one day to check it out for myself.

I entered the door and was immediately impressed to see a nice, new, shiny, and clean vet facility. I had a long conversation with the reception desk about how complicated their potential new patient would be. I was able to speak with the vet, who was a smart and very kind, younger man. I quickly went over Walter's complicated medical history and where we were now. I had been researching a new treatment for cancer I had found called Immunocidin. It was based on the "toxin therapy" of older cancer treatments, where bacteria were used to stimulate an immune response to fight cancer. I discussed our desire to use this and also to to use Fenbendazole. Fenbendazole has been used as a deworming medicine in the veterinary world for a long time. It has a good safety profile and seems to be well tolerated. There are people using this to treat cancer in their pets and refer to the "Joe Tippen protocol" as its basis. Apparently, Joe Tippen is a man who was diagnosed with advanced lung cancer who was told about Fenbendazole by one of his friends who was a vet. As the story goes, Joe Tippen went into and remained in remission by using this drug. We did a lot of online research on this related to cat and dog usage and decided to try it. We never saw any adverse reactions with using it. There does seem to be a debate on how much to give, and there obviously is a large weight discrepancy between cats, dogs, and human beings. Once again, you are left to use your best judgement and cross your fingers that it has some benefit. Fenbendazole is relatively inexpensive and apparently might have some potent "microtubule destabilizing" and positive effects against cancer cells.

The vet seemed very empathetic and stated that he certainly would be open to working with us using these new therapies. Of note, the oncologist had flat out refused to "play the middleman" when I called and inquired about using him to administer Immunocidin. A vet had to speak with and coordinate the treatment with the representative who distributed the treatment. The oncologist didn't speak to me directly; his office informed me that he didn't want to be involved. This was disappointing but not unexpected news. While the oncologist declined, this new vet was okay with attempting this new and novel treatment for cancer. I was thrilled and excited at the prospects of working with the new vet and his team. Vet Number Six was now secured, and we were going to meet with a holistic vet as well. Team Walter Strong the sequel was in full swing, and we were optimistic. We had to be optimistic.

Vet Number Seven was a very pleasant female vet. She was not the vet we were referred to; he was semi-retired and no longer seeing new patients. We sat down with her and spoke with her for about 20 minutes before she examined Walter. She felt the Immunocidin was worth a try and was also willing to do it if we wished. The new prescription was for Wei Qui Booster (Chinese herbal medicine for immune system boost) and Wei Qui Strong for assisting with weight gain. She was very optimistic that these herbal medicine capsules would have some benefit. She also wrote directions for a home cooked diet that Walter could start on. This would have no additives and would consist of a meat, chicken liver, white rice, grass fed butter, and a vegetable. We knew Walter was amongst the pickiest eaters of all time, so it was debatable if it would work. Still, we were willing to try anything. We also were given a prescription for Entyce. Entyce is an appetite stimulant primarily used in dogs and off label in cats. This was definitely not the first med we've encountered that was off label for feline usage. It really hit home that way more money and effort was channeled into canine applications than feline ones. Entyce was a grehlin receptor stimulator, which could hypothetically reverse cachexia (muscle and weight loss of cancer metabolism), which Walter most certainly had. I also inquired about milk thistle, which would provide liver support, especially since Walter was getting a high dose of Fenbendazole almost every day. She agreed with this and provided capsules. We left her office optimistic and ready to hit the kitchen for a Walter Strong home cooked meal.

The next couple of weeks were filled with home cooked meals (not for us) and a few trips to the vet. Walter decided after a few meals that the home cooked stuff was just not for him. It had to be rough after almost 16 years to eat clean. His visits for Immunocidin treatments consisted of using an ultrasound to visualize the injections into the tumor and surrounding tissue and to check progress on the tumor size after treatment.

The tumor actually appeared to shrink a little after the first few treatments, and we were all thrilled. According to their literature, Immunocidin had the ability to attack distant tumors as well as the primary ones. There was definitely evidence of mineralization within his abdominal tumor but not much change in the other tumors and lymph nodes in his omentum. Predictably, Walter did not want to eat food that contained the new Wei Qui Boost Strength formula in it. It's amazing how picky he was. I wanted to cram 10 supplements into his food, and he wanted none of it. I often thought that treating a dog would've been so much easier, considering how difficult and picky cats are in comparison.

As the tumor shrank some, so did Walter. His weight was definitely on the decline, and we were fighting like mad to keep it up. Every meal he ate was a celebration, and every missed meal was depressing.

My wife and I were on a roller coaster ride with no end in sight. The stress was palpable. We were afraid to leave him alone, so if someone had to go out of town, the other stayed at home. Our plan was to shrink this tumor to death or at least dramatically reduce its impact. We were on a race against time and weight loss. We were living in a perpetual state of stress. Life had been on a roller coaster for quite some time now.

After the fourth treatment, the vet expressed some disappointment with the latest results on the ultrasound. The tumor had actually increased some, and the local nodes and omentum tumors were also a little bigger. In my opinion, the primary tumor just needed to go. I discussed with him the potential for surgery in order to reduce the tumor's demand on his metabolic status and increasing cachexia of cancer. His weight was now in the low seven pound mark. We were losing ground now, and it scared us. I figured if we could stabilize and prop Walter up for another surgery, perhaps we could start with a cleaner slate once the tumor was removed. Our rationale with the Immunocidin treatment was to attack the cancer systemically, which, if it worked, would've been much more effective than simply removing a tumor. We knew there was cancer also in his omentum, so this strategy seemed to make sense. Did the Immunocidin have an effect on Walter's weight loss? I wondered, but there was no way to conclusively know for sure. Of course, there was a palpable risk that he could die during or after surgery. The decision tree was complicated and rife full of risk either way. I felt like it was now or never, as the clock seemed to be ticking audibly faster and louder. It was early August 2021, and we'd been at this now for at least five months post surgery.

Over the next couple of weeks, we were able to bump his weight into the mid seven pound mark. We were optimistic that we were on the right track again. We arranged to have Walter at the vet's office on the day after Labor Day for lab work, an IV for fluid volume, and then if all was okay, surgery on Tuesday. He was a little more concerned about the size of the tumor, as closing this abdominal wall was now going to be a little more difficult. Walter's activity and appetite were stable, and we actually felt comfortable enough to consider one overnight trip together for a family reunion. After much conversation and for our sanity, we decided he was looking better, and it would be safe to do an overnight. They say timing is everything. In our case, unfortunately, that was a true statement.

Our trip to see family was a long overdue event. Between the pandemic, which was now surging again due to the delta variant, and our reluctance to leave Walter alone even for a day, we were chomping at the bit. Walter had jumped on the kitchen counter several times for treats on Friday, and the timing seemed perfect. The plan was early morning Saturday departure with a return Sunday afternoon. We always worried about leaving our cats during travel and couldn't imagine coming home to anything resembling a bad outcome for one of them. There was always an underlying stress level involved with travel plans because of our "cat parent" concerns.

The trip was a true family reunion. Many of us hadn't seen each other in months due to the pandemic and there was good conversation, laughter, and of course, lots of food. We caught good weather and enjoyed the day. Saturday night we were exhausted from traveling, and by 11:00 PM we were in bed.

We were always worried about those fur babies when we traveled but had never come back to any unpleasant surprises. With that in mind, we departed around 11:00 AM on Sunday to head back home.

As my key entered the door to our home at around 3:00 PM, I was looking forward to the usual greeting. Upon opening the door, the greeting never came. Instead, we heard a loud distressing meow, with no sign of Walter or our other cats. I immediately ran upstairs when my wife yelled out, "I found Walter, he's in the kitchen."

I ran downstairs, and upon entering our kitchen, I saw Walter. He was leaning against the laundry door, his legs splayed awkwardly. He couldn't move and was crying continuously. My wife was hysterical.

"What's wrong with him?"

I picked him up and his legs flailed with no purpose. I felt his abdominal tumor, thinking perhaps it had ruptured and bled. I really did not know what this was. I did know that we needed to drop our bags and run him directly to the emergency vet clinic. We ran out the door holding him and grabbing his crate in the other arm.

Once in the car, I told my wife I thought that he either injured himself somehow or had suffered a stroke. I just kept blurting out, "This cannot be happening," as we sped down the road. We were literally one day away from starting the process of a surgery that had the potential of significantly prolonging his duration and quality of life.

Walter's head was tilted some to the left, and he was making a very strange meowing noise. At one point, I leaned over to kiss him and he nuzzled me back. This was heartbreaking. We both felt like we were in some horrific nightmare and wished we could wake up to our previous reality.

We arrived at the vet clinic and were told to wait for a vet tech to come to the car. I couldn't wait and carried Walter up to the front door. Thankfully, the door opened, and we were shown to an exam room. We gave his history to a vet tech who took Walter in to see the vet. My wife and I were crying as we awaited the veterinarian. We knew this was not going to be good.

The vet was a young lady. She appeared to be in her late twenties or early thirties. She introduced herself and informed us that she was training the vet student next to her. She then said, "I've examined Walter. He appears to have either suffered a stroke, or more likely has a large brain tumor that has probably been present all along." She went on to say, "He cannot move and appears to be totally devoid of cognition. I feel that he is not really present and is completely devoid of any cognition." She explained that she could keep him overnight to monitor him and could try an infusion of mannitol to shrink the swelling in his brain. They did not have the ability to do an MRI.

I asked her about the possibility of a stroke.

"It could be possible, but given his history, I'm strongly leaning more towards a brain tumor that is compressing on his brain causing these symptoms."

If this was it for Walter, there was no way he was spending the night away from his loving family. I asked her how we could care for him at home. My mind was reeling now. Beyond the overwhelming, crushing heartbreak, my thoughts turned to Walter's best interests. I started wondering if we might be exploring euthanasia via a home service.

"I don't think these symptoms will get better as once the tumor gets large enough. It's already compressing his brain structure. He will have to be fed with a syringe. He is past the ability to eat by himself. You will have to hold him upright to feed him."

The news just kept getting worse. I inquired about treatment in case it was a stroke.

"Could we try clot busters in case it's a stroke?"

She said she would make a call to at least cover that base.

Once the vet left the room, we balled our eyes out. I told my wife that, "It's just not supposed to end this way." I also thought about the potential of using thrombolytic drugs in case it was a stroke. You would have to give them within a relatively short time period of the event in order for them to have a chance of working. We had no idea how long ago this event happened, so it would not be feasible. Would it even be feasible since we didn't know exactly what this was and had no onsite diagnostics to help? The answer was rather obvious.

I was scrambling, just trying to think of any scenario where we could help him. We also felt extremely guilty about having left him overnight. I couldn't help but think this might not have happened if we had not gone away. We were sick, and there was not going to be any consolation.

The vet never came back in. About 20 minutes later, we were being discharged with a few anti seizure drugs to give if he seized. At this point, we just wanted to take Walter home. We were devastated. I couldn't even speak when I attempted to call my mother to let her know we made it home safely and to fill her in on the horrible news.

My wife and I started discussing the possibility of euthanizing Walter. The thought was awful, but what was his quality of life going to be? I felt betrayed as well by all the different modalities we had used in this epic fight. The cancer vaccine, all of the herbals, the immunocidin, the fenbendazole, etc. We were now just thinking that we wanted Walter to be comfortable, and we couldn't wait to get him home. I called the local "Lap of Love" office to create a file but did not commit to an appointment. The woman on the other line was extremely sympathetic, and it was comforting. We needed support, and this was a glimmer of emotional relief. We pulled into our driveway feeling defeated and crushed.

Once in our home, we held Walter on the couch, his head strangely tilted to the left. His voice was different. We wondered how this night was going to go and if he would survive until the morning. If you tried to put him down, his legs flailed hopelessly while his front arms seemed stronger. As we discussed the possibilities, Walter did a strange thing. He started purring. This was a welcome sound, but our hopes were not raised. I've read that cats can purr when happy, stressed, sick, and dying. My wife appeared next to me with a small amount of food.

"Do you think this is a good idea?" she asked.

"If we hold him straight up, it might be okay," was my answer.

There was no syringe. Walter lunged into the food with abandon. There was no difficulty eating, chewing, swallowing. We looked at each other in amazement. We watched him after he ate and continued to hold him upright to digest. We gently laid him down on his left side, which is the way his head was tilting. We then laid next to him. What happened next made us begin to question the diagnosis.

Walter nuzzled my nose, purred, kissed me all over the face, and put his paws on my cheek. For a cat who had no sign of cognition, this was a strange event. I started putting all of the events together and had a hopeful epiphany. During the car ride, he had kissed my face. When we got home he ate unassisted and without a syringe. Now, he was displaying his trademark affection. This was not the sign of a cat who was "devoid of any cognition." The decision was made for us by Walter. We were going to take him to his regularly scheduled pre op appointment at his regular vet's office first thing in the morning to get another opinion. Obviously surgery was off the table for now but he needed to be seen. We both slept downstairs with him. I slept reclined on a couch with Walter laying on my chest. My wife was next to me and asked, "Do you think he'll survive the night"?"

I didn't know but was going to attempt to be strong. I completely understand and appreciate the dilemma pet owners have when the concept and decision of euthanasia comes up. You are weighing what is best for your beloved furry friend, dealing with the guilt of playing God, and everything in between, including when is the right and appropriate time. It is a gut-wrenching thought process. We all fell asleep, not knowing what tomorrow was going to bring.

Walter wasn't much different in the morning, but he did eat again. And again, he had no issues eating. We called the vet to update them, then jumped in the car.

When the vet walked into our exam room, he looked genuinely disappointed to see Walter in this condition.

"Oh Walter, what are we going to do with you?" he said sternly.

Walter was put on the exam table and remarkably showed his trademark disdain for any vet handling. He growled, hissed, and clawed the vet's arm. The vet examined him very thoroughly and then dropped the bomb on us.

"I am not comfortable diagnosing him with a brain tumor. I'm also not thinking this was a stroke. This appears to be a spinal issue."

Walter could move all his extremities but had a dysfunction with his proprioception. The vet felt that perhaps Walter had slipped or herniated a disc in his back that was causing these issues.

"He is an older cat with some muscle wasting and malnutrition due to his cancer. He is at risk for this type of event. He could potentially have a bone tumor somewhere in his back as well. The type of cancer he has doesn't usually metastasize to bone, but cancer does what it wants."

We discussed in great depth the quality of life issues and potential for recovery.

"We have three choices. Choice one is an MRI and potential surgical consult with a neurosurgeon. I know you're not sensitive to price but this is probably $3,500 just for the MRI and involves anesthesia. Choice two is high dose steroids. If this works, you would see significant improvement in his symptoms in the next 24 to 48 hours. We all know what choice three is."

He knew we knew what choice three was. The decision was easy to make.

"I'll take what's behind door number two for $172 and a chance at recovery."

Walter received a decadron (steroid) injection, a cerenia injection for nausea, and a pain injection. We were apparently on the brink of death's door and now in a much more hopeful place. While I was disappointed Walter was not getting his surgery to remove all visible cancer, I was beyond grateful that he might recover and walk again. We were sent home with prednisolone and pain meds. Walter was sent home with a chance to continue his amazing story.

Let the waiting game begin. I was lucky enough to be off for the entire week leading into the Labor Day weekend. My wife didn't sleep a bit and had to call off from work. Her boss seemed to understand and wished her well. We had slept on the couch with Walter in shifts. I passed out holding him on my chest, and then went up to bed. My wife took the second shift. By the time we got home from the vet, we were both thoroughly exhausted.

Walter spent much of the day on his left side, and we made a point to assist him in changing positions. My wife said that he was able to roll himself enough on the egg crate with blanket on top to change positions as well.

We were waiting and praying to see some type of dramatic improvement. Pins and needles was the order of the day. He was eating well and unfortunately half of his face got full of food each time he ate. "Cleanup on aisle "seven," was heard frequently. Thank goodness for cat wipes.

It happened at around 9:00 PM. Walter was lying on the blanket when suddenly, he got himself up and took a few wobbly steps before listing and falling over. I felt like jumping for joy! This happened a few more times, and we decided, after reading some online about spinal issues in cats, to prepare a crate for him to sleep in. We didn't want him to aggravate the injury but were optimistic with his progress.

I set up an air mattress and slept next to his crate. Around 4:00 AM, my wife came down to check on him and I went up to bed for a few hours. My wife said he was holding himself up to urinate, which was also a huge step forward.

At 6:00 AM, my wife woke me up and said, "I think Walter has fluid in his lungs."

I ran downstairs, and we carefully assessed him. Using a stethoscope, I heard mostly purring noises mixed with an expiratory noise that sounded like a groan or soft meow. He was breathing some through his mouth as he purred, which concerned me.

My wife had to go into work, so I kept an eye on Walter. One of the concerns we had is that steroids can cause fluid retention. We had also given him a lot of extra water into his food to encourage hydration. After reading about this and watching videos of cats coughing online, I was convinced that he was okay. A few hours later, I listened to his lungs without him purring, and they were clear. What a relief.

My wife came home for lunch, and we decided to give him some pain medicine after she loved all over him. After she left, I was in the kitchen reading about how not to allow a recovering pet with a spinal issue jump on furniture. I was interrupted as I heard something in the living room. I ran into the room and found Walter on the couch; he had jumped on it! This was both fantastic and horrifying at the same time. I put him in the crate and realized he would require crating when not under direct supervision. The reading indicated that this type of issue can heal on its own with rest, steroids, and good nutrition. We definitely had a plan. We would give him time out of the crate supervised and would crate him when unsupervised.

It was now around 10:00 PM. We were all watching TV in the living room. To our amazement, Walter got up, took a few quick running steps, and was back in the crate. We watched with a sense of amazement as he held himself up to relieve himself. Wow, this had been some 36 hours of progress! We were very hopeful Walter was on his way to full function, and our fingers were crossed.

Tuesday through Thursday saw incremental improvement. There was still some radical imbalance to his gait but also some steps appeared normal at times. We saw no signs or symptoms of seizures and no signs of distress. His purr was completely abnormal; it was a high pitched inspiratory noise, which sounded like stridor. The expiration was normal purring, and there was an occasional huffing noise, which sounded like a cough. Since his normal non-purring breathing appeared normal, we were reassured but completely confused.

Friday, I had to take one of our other cats to the vet for a non-resolving mouth infection. After we discussed her revised plan of care, the vet said, "I know you want to ask me some questions about Walter. I can see it in your face." He really knew how to read an audience.

I asked him about the possibility of a brain tumor (unlikely based on his rapid response to steroids and continued improvement), the plan of care (crating while unsupervised was good), a plan to start weaning the high dose of prednisolone, and if we could still potentially proceed with a revision surgery down the road if a resolution of current issue occurs to remove all visible cancer from his abdomen (absolutely). I couldn't stand the fact that he still had tumors in his abdomen; I felt like removing them would comfortably extend his life. My entire week of vacation was spent running a cat ICU where I had two patients to look after. I felt like a patient myself after a few days of this and told my wife that a "psych consult" would be appropriate. I felt depressed and trapped in the house. I was grateful to be off so that I could help with his care but also disappointed that it devoured a huge chunk of my off time.

I realized that I was being completely consumed with Walter's condition and care. The feeling was one of determination mixed with absolute exhaustion. I sometimes wondered if my wife and I had morphed into crazy cat people. I guess we were both guilty of caring probably more than most "normal" people. I guess it's hard to define normal, but one thing's for sure: We viewed these cats as family.

We had to make light of this situation as we were both feeling the weight of involvement, stress, and sadness. We decided that since Walter was making steady progress, we would accept this as great news and could only look forward. No sense in trying to control what, obviously, we had no control over. We would do our best.

While Walter walked out into our courtyard with the occasional unsteady gait to sunbath, we marveled at his strength, perseverance, and bravery. We watched him and wondered what his follow up appointment would bring.

The days leading up to the follow up appointment were concerning. We were completely exhausted from the constant stress, and Walter was lethargic. His weight measured seven pounds, the lowest he had ever weighed in his adult life. His gait was better, but he still had missteps and sometimes lost his balance. More concerning yet was his temp, which hovered around 102.5, which is right on the brink of a fever. We were convinced he needed antibiotics, as his purr sounded congested with a high-pitched strider at times and an occasional sneeze or cough. When I was greeted by his vet on September 9, I presented him a video of the bizarre "purr in question." Walter would never purr in a vet's office; he would be more apt to bite or scratch a member of the staff. The vet also found his purring strange and decided that antibiotics, anti-nausea meds, and subcutaneous fluids were appropriate. Walter had a chest X-ray, which showed a small area of concern.

"It might be an infection or it could be something worse." We knew something worse could mean lung cancer. We hoped for the best, but this gave us more cause for concern. One hopeful sign that this could be infection was the staining on Walter's face, which was pretty profound. We would clean his face, and hours later, it would be filthy. We assumed food, but the vet thought drainage. We also discussed the possibility of further surgery, as he thought the abdominal tumor felt a tad bigger on this exam. We were continuing Fenbendazole but knew that removal of this awful tumor would give him the best chance.

"He is too high risk now, but let's give him some time to recover from whatever this is, and then we can reassess the surgery."

The clock was ticking. We were praying for a rapid resolution of whatever this was. We had to remain Walter Strong.

The days after his visit were challenging. We cleaned that little stained face several times a day and decided to increase his boundaries. His mobility was improved but not quite normal. The attempt to re-introduce him to pre-incident life was in full swing. His appetite was also challenging with a weight that vacillated between seven and eight pounds.

Watching this thin, dirty-faced cat who no longer was grooming himself has heartbreaking. How long would it be this way, and how long did we have before surgery and/or improvement was no longer a possibility? We didn't know and were trying to cope as best we could. I purchased steps to help him into and out of our bed. The steps were quickly ignored as he jumped off the bed and landed on the floor, looking unsure and somewhat unsteady. I knew to save the receipt on those steps, as I had a feeling he wouldn't use them. I'd just add them to the collection of Walter assisted mobility device rejects. They would be right next to the ramp I had purchased seven months ago for his surgery. I suppose dogs are more apt to use these things. Walter probably laughed at us and our frivolous attempts to guide him into compliant patient status.

September 12, 2021. The start of football season for a Steeler fan. I was so grateful to have my little buddy with us to watch the game. I woke up, had a long breakfast complete with lots of strong coffee, and sat in the courtyard with our cats. Walter had already eaten a few times this morning. He had Fenbendazole, mushrooms, and Dasaquin mixed into his food. The strangest thing he was currently doing was still an occasional higher pitched purr with a cough or sneeze. We added a lysine gel to his regimen in case he had a viral infection that was causing this. As I reflected, 'I was thinking Walter probably had been battling this cancer anywhere from 12 to 16 months already.

I had a short cry that morning, thinking about how much he had been through. The strength and love that this cat exuded was truly something to behold. I firmly believe only cat people are truly in tune with these vibes; very profound stuff for sure.

Giving meds to a cat is a challenging task, and as their appetite wanes, it becomes even harder. I was amazed we were able to sneak as many things into his food as we were. We were almost finished with the weaning of his prednisolone dose, and my wife now had him licking it from the cap of the bottle. This was the only easy medicine that we had to administer. Thank goodness for a small victory.

Over the next couple of days, Walter's mobility stabilized. He still had an occasional slip or sideway step, but overall, he was much better. A bigger concern, however, was the size of his abdominal tumor. There was no doubt it had gotten a little bigger, and we were now feeling pressured to act. The situation seemed to boil down to a choice: Either we might have to risk having a surgery to remove all visible cancerous tumor, or he would continue to deteriorate and would die a slow, miserable death. We had come this far, and the thought of a slow miserable death was not an option. We made an appointment with his primary vet for a re-exam for Friday, which was the fastest we could get him in. Our goal in doing this was to have a diagnostic idea of where his cancer stood. X-rays, lab work, etc., were going to be on the table for this visit. While hardly at his peak physical form, we were hopeful that Walter would survive a second surgery, which might grant him more time to have quality of life.

Conversely, the possibility of Walter passing away during or after surgery was certainly a real possibility.

We were desperately trying to feed him as much as we could, and it was difficult. He was also now receiving lysine, as we all thought he had a viral upper respiratory issue. His once white face was now constantly stained with eye drainage, and "cleanup on aisle seven" happened once a day on this poor cat's face. Stressed or not and ready or not, Friday was coming, and we would have a better idea of where we stood on this battle with his cancer.

Driving to the vet felt like stepping out onto the plank before you are expected to drop into the cold, unforgiving waters below. Inherently, I had a feeling that this was not going to be a good-news-bearing visit. I was so anxious that I needed to step out a few times to use the restroom. Each time I went to leave the exam room, Walter looked over at me and started meowing incessantly. This was utter heartbreak. He was scared, and so was I.

The vet examined Walter and stated that his tumor felt larger. I asked if he felt any fluid, and he said no.

We discussed what a potential surgery would consist of if Walter was going to be a surgical candidate. The mass now took up about 40 percent of the abdominal width. He felt like mesh would have to be incorporated.

Walter, to his surprise, was not fighting him as much during the exam. I knew this was not a good sign. He stated that Walter's ears and gums looked a little pale. The plan was now to get an ultrasound requiring sedation, full chest and thoracic X-rays, and comprehensive lab work.

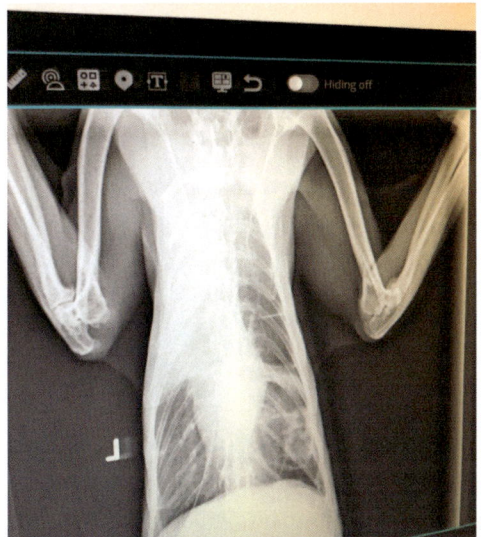

Before they took Walter back, we had a frank discussion about the plan. I felt like if Walter was a surgical candidate, then full steam ahead. If the diagnostic work found more ominous findings, we could potentially treat with more Immunocidin and perhaps steroids. The vet felt this was reasonable, and I left with my heart tucked insecurely in my throat.

After crying on the way home, I cried more once I reached the house. This was a grueling couple of hours, waiting on a phone call that actually didn't come. I called around 12:30 because I had a 1:00 PM appointment and was told that the vet wanted to speak with me on the phone at some point later. I informed the receptionist that I would just show up at around 2:00 PM.

I arrived at 2:00 and felt like the proverbial Charlie Brown cloud was descending over my head. I entered the exam room and waited for the vet. He walked in and was holding a vial full of a white liquid.

"Walter is not going to be a surgical candidate," he said, and I braced myself for the worst. "Walter is pretty anemic. His last hematocrit was 30 now it's down to 23. I will pull up the X-rays. The area that we were unsure about in his lungs has grown. Based on his history, I have to assume its metastatic cancer. There is also fluid in one of his lobes. In addition, his abdomen has ascitic fluid in it, and when I went to get a urine sample through his abdomen, this white ascitic fluid came out, much to my displeasure. His mesentery is floating in fluid, and draining it won't do much good because it will just fill back up."

I knew that this meant the cancer was in its final stages. I could feel my heart breaking into a thousand pieces.

"Walter did not tolerate the sedation well. He stiffened up at one point, which was very odd."

It just kept getting worse. I asked how long he felt Walter had left.

"Is it days?" I asked.

"I would think weeks, maybe longer, but you never know," was his answer.

I felt the blood running out of my face.

"So what is the plan?" I managed the squeak out of my mouth, voice somewhat breaking.

"Well, surgery is not an option. I did give a good dose of Immunocidin into his abdominal tumor and also injected depo-medrol as well."

I found this odd because steroids are not recommended with this drug, as it potentially could cancel out the interleukin immune response.

"I'm not seeing a lot of evidence in the literature to state that in cats and because this is more used in dogs, it is debatable. I didn't inject them in the same location."

This vet was very good at communicating, and it was appreciated.

It took everything I had to maintain my calm train of thought.

"How about intravenously administering the Immunocidin for a systemic attempt?" I offered.

"I thought about that," he replied. "To be honest, it makes me kind of nervous to administer something used for intratumoral injection intravenously, but we might be at the end of our rope'."

He was correct, the rope in fact was now slipping out of Team Walter Strong's hands.

"WTF do we have to lose at this point?" was my answer.

"Shit, why not?" was his response.

We both knew there was a protocol for this route, but it would carry a potential greater risk. We discussed the possibility that this treatment could potentially cause a bad outcome and kill him. I also inquired about anything to help his work of breathing with fluid in his lungs and suggested lasix as an option.

"I'm not sure it'll offer much benefit, but at this point, why not? Perhaps if will offer some benefit."

I dropped my head and told the vet that I felt like I had failed Walter. The vet looked at me incredulously and said, "It would be impossible for you to have tried any harder for Walter. You have done a thousand times more than most people could have done."

I appreciated the words but still felt like a failure. It seemed my beloved friend was dying, and I now felt somewhat helpless to save him.

I was so happy to see Walter coming out in his familiar blue crate. He was still growling from all the poking and prodding, but he stopped growling when he saw my familiar face. I paid the large bill and put Walter into the back of my car.

The phone call to my wife was brutal. There was so much crying that it was hard to make out what was being said. I hated to update her with this catastrophic news, but I would want to know and figured she would, too. I cried really hard all the way home.

When I got home, I fed Walter, who surprisingly seemed hungry. I then held him real close and told him how much I loved him and how proud I was of his bravery. It was truly galling to know that this beautiful and loving cat had normal liver, kidney, and heart function but was being ravaged by this relentless cancer. I couldn't help but think back to last year at this time when his diagnosis was being missed by the cat clinic. If only they had appropriately considered cancer earlier as a differential diagnosis in an older cat with chronic abdominal inflammation and weight loss, we probably could have removed a small non metastatic adenocarcinoma, which might have been curative. It really made me sick to my stomach to think about this.

I then told Walter that we weren't done. You see, to be Walter Strong means you don't quit. You fight until there is no more fighting left to do. I would fight for Walter until my last breath. If Walter was up for the fight, I'd be right next to him, battling to the end. Death was knocking on the door, but until it broke the door down, we were going to attempt to kick its ass. My wife felt the same way, and we spoke about what we had left to offer Walter in his treatment.

The plan was to let Walter rest a few days while getting lasix every 12 hours in an attempt to control via diuresis, the fluid in his lungs. We ran out and purchased a new batch of powdered medicinal mushrooms and krill oil, which has antioxidant and anti-inflammatory effects. We were going to double his Fenbendazole dosage. Amazingly, his liver and kidney function was still normal despite what was going on in his abdomen. The vet had recommended restarting prednisolone every other day, but we decided to hold off for now because of the Immunocidin. This decision was based on a conversation I had with the distributor of Immunocidin, who was also a vet. He stated that steroids given concurrently would prevent the interleukin release, which would inactivate the immune response. He also recommended the route of administration being changed to intraperitoneal instead of intravenous. I thanked him for his time, and to my amazement, he confided in me that he himself was now battling metastatic cancer. I felt terrible for him and felt compelled to share what I had learned about Fenbendazole as an adjunct treatment. This was a sad and informative conversation. I wished him the best in his recovery and said I'd pray for him.

I called the vet's office and left a message for him to contact the Immunocidin vet in order to coordinate the best course of action. We were certainly down but not out. If Walter still showed the will to fight, we would fight for him.

September 19, 2021. Last night was the first night in a while that my sweet cat spent the night cuddled up next to me. He would get under the covers, make sure my arm was around him, then put his face in mine and purr himself off to sleep. This happened as a cycle all night, as he would get up to urinate and then return to the bed. The lasix was diuresing him, but no one knew how much, if any, impact it had on his lung or abdominal fluid. He actually had a decent breakfast, complete with additional vitamins and Fenbendazole. I had found a research study involving cats with lung cancer that had been receiving IB-DNQ (isobutyl-deoxynyboqinone) as part of a research study at a veterinary school in Illinois. Of course, I called and emailed to see if I could get Walter involved. We were at the point of trying anything to save him. In the interim we would shower him with love affection and as much food as he wanted.

Our weekend was basically reduced to cat ICU and cancer ward. One of our other cats, our 18-year-old cat Simba, was now on her fourth antibiotic for a mouth infection post multi extraction of teeth. She was not doing terribly well either. My wife and I took a long walk and discussed what a long and glorious life these cats all have had. They received lots of love, the best food and medical attention, and even had the opportunity to live in a few different states. We catered to their every need, and in return, they showed us beautiful unconditional love and provided companionship. Conversations like these were important to have, as they allowed us to see through the grief and visualize the big picture. Of course, the sadness and impending sense of doom were ever present, but reflections like this provided a little relief.

We decided to investigate a local support group for grieving pet owners. We figured it couldn't hurt. We were still actively engaged in fighting the fight but felt like additional support would be helpful. We had to also take care of ourselves, and Walter needed us to be strong for him. We were less worried about Simba, as clinically she was doing well except for swelling on one side of her face.

The next couple of days were very hit and miss...mostly miss. Walter was successfully diuresing, but the loss of fluid and subsequent volume left him looking dehydrated and weaker. We encouraged him to eat and drink as much as possible, but it was difficult. We knew that without appetite stimulants, he would go down quickly, and they weren't working as well at this point. My intention was to get Walter into the vet office for more Immunocidin treatment either intratumoral, intravenously, or intraperitoneal. My thought process was that if we could kill off some of the cancer, his overall condition could improve. The cachexia of cancer was really working against us, and the clock was starting to tick quicker.

Thursday, September 23, found Walter looking especially rundown. His energy level was really low, and his appetite was poor despite our best efforts. I was watching him lose muscle mass and weight at an alarming rate. I cancelled his appointment for Immunocidin and decided later in the day to seek a vet visit. Being that my appointment with the vet was already cancelled, I rolled the dice and negotiated a last-minute appointment at another vet's office.

Walter offered little resistance as I tucked him into the cat carrier and went zooming down the road.

The vet was a pleasant young lady with a lovely bedside manner. She sat on the floor and petted Walter as she examined him. Her gentleness and calm demeanor made both of us feel at ease.

Walter got on the scale and weighed 6.2 pounds. I gasped as my once 13-pound cat was now evaporating before my eyes.

She repeated his chest X-ray and flashed un ultrasound over his abdomen. The X-ray looked similar to his previous, and she was not sure if it was pneumonia or metastatic lung cancer. She did not find much in the way of ascitic fluid in his abdomen, which was a relief. Her plan was to give him some subcutaneous fluid, add gabapentin for pain and appetite stimulation, and put him on antibiotics in case he had bacterial pneumonia. She also prescribed Flagyl, as he was having loose bowel movements. His abdominal film showed that he was constipated, so they gave him two enemas and added lactulose to soften his stool. It was all so overwhelming on top of an already overwhelming clinical picture.

I had been researching an herbal supplement called Arteminisin, which many holistic vets used to assist with cancer. It acts by attaching to the iron of rapidly dividing cells (cancer), thus killing the cell by subtracting the iron. I had read about this but was concerned about some truly horrific adverse outcomes some people had with it, mostly in dogs. At this point, I thought of the scene in the movie *Jaws* where they get ready to lower the shark cage in a last ditch effort to kill the shark. This was going to be Walter's last chance to turn the corner and defeat his shark; the rotten cancer that was eating him alive. The vet was fine with adding this to his extensive regimen.

We got home and tried to be optimistic. As long as we had hope and Walter has willing to fight, we carried on.

Walter didn't produce a solid stool at the vet's, and after leaving him there for several hours, we took him home. The rest of our day consisted of cheering for a solid poop. We were greeting explosive diarrhea instead. In fact, there were several bouts of this. The directions were to bring him back the next day for reexamination if he hadn't pooped. We had a friend visiting from out of town, and he knew Walter well. During a previous visit, apparently Walter had planted a "shit bomb" on the bathroom rug, and our friend stepped in it unknowingly. These two had never really cared for each other, so I'm sure Walter knew exactly what he was doing. He was now referred to as "Shit Foot Cat" by our friend.

We tried to entertain our friend during the weekend as best we could, but our minds were always on Walter. On Friday, we took him back to the vet, and she repeated his X-ray. Thankfully, he now had an empty colon, so the plan had worked. We were now giving Walter two different appetite stimulants—Mirataz and Entyce—and Gabapentin for pain. We also were giving him additional pain medicine if he looked uncomfortable. His weekend was actually decent, as he spent time outside in our courtyard and slept in the bed with us some, which was glorious.

Unfortunately, Walter's weekend rally was short-lived. His appetite and energy level both declined in a radical fashion as the week went on. We were trying everything to get him to eat more, but he just wouldn't eat enough to maintain his metabolic needs. This cancer was stealing his nutrients, and his muscle mass was continuing to waste away. I had an appointment for Immunocidin Friday if he was up to it. My hope was that he would catch a second wind and turn the corner.

It was heartbreaking to attempt pilling him. I had figured out that using tiny empty gel caps to deliver his meds were the easiest and most efficient way of delivering the medicine. Unfortunately, Walter didn't agree, and it was always difficult to pill him. My wife and I felt terrible watching him struggle against getting the pills or liquid meds he needed. It was hard knowing that he really didn't seem interested in participating in our regimen. We felt guilty, in a way, for putting him through something that he hated. We also knew if we did nothing, then he would stand no chance of survival. We were about to truly find out where Walter's boundaries stood.

Thursday, September 30, will go down as one of the worst days of my life. My wife woke me up and told me that Walter has not doing well. She had spent the night on the couch downstairs with him and informed me that he had vomited and wasn't breathing very well. We listened to his breath sounds, which were normal, but he was crying a lot and seemed uncomfortable. More concerning yet was his energy level; he didn't have one. He could barely take a step before lying down. In addition, his temperature was 94 degrees. The normal temp for a cat was 99.5 to 102.5. He was hypothermic and needed to be actively warmed. I wondered if we could raise his temp and relieve some of his lethargy, loss of appetite, and make him feel a little better.

This was a new low for Walter's condition. He was very limp when you held him, and he seemed like his gas tank was on empty. My wife decided to call out of work to stay with him, and it killed me to have to go to work.

She began actively warming him with a heating pad, blankets, and a hot pad. You had to be careful not to burn him, so all of these were covered with towels.

I cried all the way to work, and my wife was crying on the other line as she updated me. I suggested that she take him to the vet if he didn't perk up, and she agreed. We also were now thinking that we might have to put the hospice folks on call, just in case. Our hearts were heavy as my wife made a 1:00 PM appointment with the vet.

You cannot imagine how hard it was to provide anesthesia while your mind was reeling with what we were dealing with at home. However, my mind was always able to focus sharply on my work, and I actually welcomed the distraction. My wife updated me frequently on Walter's status, and our stress level was high as he was not doing well at all. She had managed to increase his temp to 99, which was now in the normal range. I was lucky to be at lunch when my wife arrived at the vet. I was put on speaker phone as the vet examined him.

"Walter has changed dramatically since the last time I saw him. He has actually lost another pound and now weighs 5.2 pounds. He seems very tired, and I feel like he is telling us that he is ready. I can do X-rays and give fluid, but I don't think it will make much of a difference. You are great cat parents, and I can tell you that if this was my kitty, I would call the hospice vet today."

Wow. This was not the news anyone wanted to hear. I was sick to my stomach as I heard my wife sobbing hard on the other line. With a heavy heart, I went to start another case.

At around 3:30, my wife texted me a video and informed me that Walter was now mouth breathing and his lips appeared blue. I felt a cold sweat run down my back and immediately asked my chief to come into my room. I showed her the text and said that I needed to go home immediately. Luckily, there was someone available to relieve me, and I bolted out of the hospital as fast as I could.

I cried so hard on the way home that it was hard to see the road in front of me. Walter was dying, and I needed to be with him. Earlier in the day, my wife and I discussed attempting to spend one last night with Walter to shower him with love. Now, the hard and cruel reality was that these were going to be our last few hours together. I was crushed, defeated, and sad beyond measure.

With tears streaming down my face, I rushed out of my car once I reached the driveway and ran into our house.

My wife was holding Walter on her lap with a towel wrapped around him. He was absolutely lifeless and looked like skin and bones. When we lived in Georgia, I once watched Walter take a running jump onto a seven-foot fence and land on it perfectly balanced. He was acrobatic most of his life and ran like a greyhound at the track. Now, he could barely hold his head up. He occasionally let out a hellacious meow and wasn't breathing normally. His abdomen was heaving, and in between, he was mouth breathing on occasion. I kissed him, and my wife handed him to me."

I couldn't believe this was my cat who just a few weeks ago was 7.5 pounds. He was gaunt and was unable to hold up his head without assistance. I had read that when cats go downhill, it happens quickly, as they are very stoic and usually can hide illness very well. There was no hiding what was happening now. Walter was dying in front of our eyes, and it was painfully difficult to watch. I sat with him on the couch as my wife pleaded with the hospice vet to arrive ASAP. It was obvious our beloved cat had only minutes to live at this point. With tears pouring down my face, I kissed and held him close. He would rest and then let out a torrent of loud meows. What a helpless feeling knowing we couldn't do anything to help him. Finally, I asked my wife to draw up a dose of Buporphrenone to give him. It is an opioid pain med for cats. I couldn't stand to see him suffering in this condition, and we needed something to relax him and relieve his condition. I knew that this medicine could also cause his respirations to slow, and at this point that would be okay, as he was breathing rapidly. I was pretty sure Walter's last breath would occur before the hospice person would arrive. Truthfully, Walter was in his lap of love; he was surrounded by the people who adored him and loved him more than anything.

At around 5:00 PM, Walter's respirations were getting very shallow. I could feel him twitching with an increasing frequency, which I assumed could be seizure activity. I'm quite sure he had been hypoxic for quite a while now and believed that his brain was hypoxic as well. My hope is that he was unaware of what was currently happening, and I believe he was. He let out one last loud yelp, then began gasping for air. My wife couldn't bear to watch this, and she ran out of the room to vomit. She came back in a few seconds later, and Walter quietly took his last few breaths. He was gone.

We held him and cried our eyes out, knowing that our beloved baby had crossed the rainbow bridge and was in heaven. There is no way to truly express how much this hurt. We were hoping for a quiet, dignified euthanasia for Walter, but he had other ideas. I figured that Walter died on his own terms, which is how he lived his whole life. He was a strong-willed, beautiful cat who was the king of his own jungle; he was the alpha cat in our house, and he knew it. We held him for several minutes and just admired how beautiful he was, even in death. I didn't want to ever let him go.

It dawned on us that Walter had probably been actively dying throughout the last 24 hours. Our lifelong bond was so strong that I believe he held on and waited for me to get home to be with him before he finally let himself go. It was both heartbreaking and beautiful to think this way. Our beloved and adored Walter had passed away, and life would not be the same without him. Our hearts were broken, and while we knew Walter would always live on in our hearts, the pain and agony were unbearable.

The hospice vet arrived, and we updated her on the ill-timed passing of our beloved cat. She took an impression of his paw in clay, clipped a locket of his hair, and spent time speaking with us. She was amazed at how hard we fought for him and consoled us. I couldn't help but think that I could never do her job. It would be far too sad for me to ever witness the death of these beautiful creatures on a regular basis. In a sense, I had an overwhelming feeling of failure. A lot of "what ifs" crept into my head. What if we had done an earlier re-excision surgery, say back in May when he was still strong? What if we chose to do the surgery instead of systemically treating him with Immunocidin? What if we had never chose the cat clinic as our vet and someone else diagnosed this earlier before it had a chance to spread?

This was a cruel and torturous way to think, so I decided to pull the plug on these thoughts. We made the best decisions for Walter based on what we knew. It is certainly possible that Walter may not have survived another surgery or could have had catastrophic complications even if he did. It was also possible that this cancer could have been in multiple other places, and if so, it would've been cruel to put him through a surgery that was never going to be curative. Back in January, we were told that Walter's cancer was late stage. They had given him a two month prognosis after his surgery in early February. Walter lived eight months post surgery. Seven of those months, he enjoyed a fairly good quality of life. The last month, his quality of life declined and then declined precipitously towards the end. We had done the best we could, but we were more proud of Walter's bravery, toughness, and love. I feel like we all wanted to be together for as long as possible, and the fight for life reflected this.

The end of our proceeding consisted of me carrying Walter in a basket to the hospice vet's car. This was so incredibly difficult, as my wife and I really didn't want him to ever leave us. The vet kindly informed us that, "Your baby will come back to you in a beautiful urn and will be with your forever."

In my mind, I was hopeful that when my time for afterlife came, I would be reunited with Walter again.

Realizing neither one of us had eaten, my wife and I picked up the pieces and went to dinner. Neither one of us were really hungry but needed to get out of the house. We reminisced about what a beautiful life Walter had with us and how hard we fought to save his life. In a sense, our #WalterStrong commitment drew us closer to Walter and also closer to each other. Walter's bravery and strength was inspiring, and his fighting spirit right down to the bitter end was vintage Walter. He was a beautiful and brave, free spirit who we had the privilege of having in our lives for 16 years. He left us too soon, but we are grateful that he now rests in peace. Till we meet again, we love you, Walter.

The days following this event were brutal. My heart would beat, and I could imagine a lot of the blood leaking out around the hole that was now in my heart. We cried several times a day and felt like we were wandering aimlessly about much of the time. We were allowing ourselves to grieve, but no matter how many tears were shed, the pain remained. The house felt empty as we expected to see Walter greet us in the courtyard when we came home or pop his little head out between the bannisters to steal a look at us on the couch. Our other two cats seemed especially needy. Walter's brother Mayfield seemed on the depressed side and was much quieter than usual. All told, we were all grieving in a house that was now devoid of its majestic centerpiece. We were going to have to learn how to live in this new world that just seemed a tad colder and emptier. They say time heals all, but when you're wallowing in fresh grief, it provides little consolation.'

We tried to focus on Walter's long, beautiful life instead of his quick and unsightly death. The road to recovery was painful, and we wondered how long until we felt normal. The only thing that gave us comfort was the fact that Walter was no longer suffering. For this, we were grateful. We were also proud of him and of ourselves for putting up such a heroic fight.

I'd like to make some observations and suggestions to pet owners. The incidence of cancer is way too high in both dogs and cats. Think PREVENTION. Based on our experience and my research into similar experiences pet owners have had, I'd recommend starting with diet. It would appear that there are limitless food choices for pet owners to choose from. I would spend the extra money to buy the highest quality food you can afford. In addition, I would add any sources of additional antioxidants (species appropriate vegetables) into their food. Find a progressive and well-rounded vet who can actually provide guidance on this. If they don't dabble in nutritional counseling, perhaps consider a vet who does. I mention nutrition first because its the first thing I think of when I think of cancer rates in these beautiful animals. Humans consume certain foods that have been linked to potential cancer development, so why would it be different in animals? I would discuss with your vet possibly cycling some supplements such as coenzyme Q10 or an immune system supporting supplement into their food. There are many immune stimulating mushroom powders out there to try. Bone broth is another suggestion, as there is research supporting its benefit to the immune system. Proviable or other digestive health supplements may be beneficial. Make informed choices based on researching things for yourself. I never fully bought into on-line advertisements for "cancer cures" but rather read how people handled these situations when faced with them. Forums such as Facebook cancer support groups for animals would be a good place to start, as these people are not attempting to make money; they are merely sharing advice that may have worked for them.

You have to educate yourself on different treatment modalities and options in conjunction with your vet. Part of this is asking questions and coming up with a plan that is reasonable and makes sense. Think PREVENTION. For dogs and cats who are entering their senior years, I would advise being proactive with your vet. For example, why not suggest an abdominal ultrasound if your senior dog or cat is having GI issues? Think EARLY diagnosis. The cat clinic we used treated Walter for IBD and pancreatitis without considering cancer, which is very prevalent in older cats. If our cat clinic had suggested this earlier, Walter would probably be sitting on this desk watching me write a book about anything other than his fight for survival and untimely death. Be involved in your pets' care. Treat them like family because they are family. I would say that when you adopt that puppy or kitten, you are making a commitment to them. That commitment should include a yearly vet visit and proper medical care when needed. It should also include picking a really good vet. The initial vet we chose fell asleep at the wheel for months and treated Walter for IBD and pancreatitis, all while ignoring the possibility of cancer. If I could go back in time, I would run from this practice. In retrospect, I would imagine most competent vets would've acted a lot earlier and faster given his age and symptoms. If you can't make that commitment, then maybe let someone else adopt the pet instead. This sounds harsh, but dogs and cats are not property; they are living, feeling, beautiful creatures. They need to be treated with love and respect.

When it comes to cancer as a diagnosis, there are some treatment options. Surgery, chemotherapy, and radiation come to mind. Seek out an oncologist who is progressive. There are many different kinds of cancer, and each might have a different treatment option. All these options are expensive to a degree.

This is why prevention and early detection are so important. Some cancers, if caught early enough, are curable. Once the metastasis train starts, it's very hard to derail it. Trust me, we tried everything. Your money is better spent trying to prevent and early detect this before it starts.

Faced with an aggressive cancer diagnosis, we chose to throw the kitchen sink at it. We were able to quadruple Walter's poor prognosis time. A large majority of the treatments I found were online participating in the forums. I also did a lot of research. Please note: The miracle cancer cures some unscrupulous companies tout tend to pray on people's emotions in order to profit. Educate yourselves. We used a host of supplements such as medicinal mushrooms, Chinese herbal medicine, IP6, Artenimisin, COQ10, fish oil, krill oil, Fenbendazole, etc. There are many supplements out there that people have used successfully. Your vet or oncology vet may not be in favor of trying these things. Use your discretion. In late-stage cancer, I don't see the downside of trying things, as long as they do not cause further harm or discomfort to your beloved pet. I found the Torigen vaccine and Immunocidin via online search and researching. It's truly hard to know how to combine these modalities together, so a lot of it is unfortunately trial and error. In addition, it's hard to know which one of the modalities actually worked. That is certainly the frustrating part of using more than one treatment modality.

It pains me to say, but I believe dogs might be easier to treat than cats. Cats are extraordinarily difficult to medicate. They are difficult to pill, don't like liquid squirted in their mouth, are very picky eaters, and know when you are sneaking meds into their food. I can't imagine using a pill pocket, for example, for a cat (I'm sure someone out there has had success with this, but this wouldn't work for us). I've seen people use peanut butter to deliver meds to a dog; could you imagine the horror on a cat's face if offered a big glob of peanut butter? Not happening!

We were extremely frustrated with our inability to provide Walter with as many of the supplements we had on hand for him because of his lack of cooperating with the delivery method. We attempted mixing things in baby food for a while until he caught on. If you mixed meds in his food, he would walk away. If you then presented regular food, he'd eat it. They just have a great sense of smell, and they are smarter than you think. I was able to mix

IP6 in cat sip, which is a lactose free milk for cats. This was one of the few things that was tasteless. Fenbendazole is also tasteless and was easy to mix the granules in food. Coenzyme Q10 was also tolerated in food. Most other supplements or meds were met with a quick rejection. It's definitely worth trying, as each cat is remarkably different.

Shortly after Walter's death, we noticed profound changes in his sister cat Simba. She had undergone a dental procedure about two months prior and wasn't healing. After having eight teeth removed and a gum flap surgery, she was on her fifth antibiotic. We decided to switch vets to get a fresh pair of eyes on her. The cat who was now 17 and never sick a day in her life was now diagnosed with squamous cell carcinoma of her mouth. It's a cruel form of aggressive cancer, and with this late diagnosis, it was not looking like she would have long to live. We were still grieving Walter, and bang, here we go again.

Literally, eight days after Walter's death, his sister cat Simba also passed away. While still devastated with Walter's passing, we were completely overwhelmed with another family member's death. The daily crying sessions only intensified for both of us. I'd like to think they would at least take comfort in having each other's company in heaven. Truth is, they didn't like each other in this life. I could imagine her getting up there and both of them looking at each and muttering, "Oh shit, it's you." I hope the reality is they are happy to see each other and have made friends in the afterlife. I take comfort knowing we will see them again when our time comes.

I was hoping to be writing this book for years to come about how Walter had defied the odds and beat an awful metastatic cancer. Despite our best efforts, it was not to be. I had mentioned earlier in this book about our poor experience with a local vet multi-specialty clinic. We thought a lot about Walter's course of misdiagnosis and all the associated wasted time in 2020 into 2021. Was Walter's cancer potentially curative if it had been detected and diagnosed earlier? There was now plenty of time to dissect this. How did we get here? After a small period of reflection and a request for medical records from the initial cat clinic, we knew the answer...and it was not good.

The medical records never lie. This is a fact in medicine or veterinary medicine. We began to review his medical records. In July 2020, Walter had been noted to have progressive weight loss, a long-standing history of GI issues, especially constipation, and other symptoms. His medical records stated he had a history of megacolon, which was, in fact, not true. This was disappointing and, to us, reflected either an oversight or just plain sloppiness. What was more concerning as we reviewed his records is that they actually mentioned cancer as a potential differential diagnosis and didn't mention this to us. Worse, they did not address the possibility of cancer in his diagnostic tests or treatment plan. They drew labs and then diagnosed him with pancreatitis and IBD. The problem with this in retrospect is that IBD can mimic lymphoma. In fact, all of these symptoms can be suggestive of lymphoma or other types of gastrointestinal cancers. If we could go back in time, I would've gotten up and screamed, "Let's do an ultrasound!" but we just didn't know enough back then to question much. The vast majority of what we have learned was on the fly, and we just kept on researching and learning 14 months later. On the cat clinic's own website they have a section that expressed how important and potentially lifesaving early detection and diagnosis is in cats. They might advertise this, but in the case of our beloved cat, they failed to follow their own advice.

I would remiss if I didn't address the age issue here. What is the average age of a cat? Were we being vastly unrealistic? Seems like on average perhaps 14 to 16. If you look deeper into this, there are cats that live well into their twenties. The oldest living cat was either in his late twenties or thirties. To us, the issue was co-existing disease and quality of life. Walter had no other acute issues. I always thought his kidneys would fail as they do in older cats. At the time of his death, his values were still normal. I'm sure he had arthritis like any cranky old man would, but overall, he was looking like a long gamer. We were praying that would be the case. Being old in and of himself shouldn't be seen as a disease, whether cat nor man. We don't stop treating healthy older people when you they get sick, so why should it be different for your furry family member?

Everything we have read about IBD, pancreatitis, and feline gastrointestinal cancer suggest using appropriate diagnostic tests. These would include an abdominal ultrasound, CT scan, endoscopy with potential biopsy, and radiographs (X-ray). This is not to suggest all of these tests are ordered, but they are the ones most appropriate for early detection. Even one of these tests back in July 2020 very likely would've caught his cancer early. This clinic did not order a single one of these and did not refer us to a specialist until four months had gone by. During that time period, Walter's condition progressively deteriorated despite our constant phone conversations and updates with the clinic. We were crossing our fingers, mixing pumpkin in his food, giving steroids, and wondering why his IBD and pancreatitis were not getting better.

In fact, Walter's repeat labs at his follow up visit at the end of October 2020 were catastrophically worse than his labs in early July. The picture was becoming very clear to us. They had simply diagnosed Walter and prescribed him medication without taking the time to support the diagnosis with appropriate diagnostic work.

As we worked through the scenarios, we got more and more despondent. I felt like I had failed Walter. After all, I'm in the medical field, and surely, I should've hit the alarm bell and yanked him out of that clinic in July. My wife had to remind me that I'm not a veterinarian, oncologist, time traveler, or a fortune teller. We had relied on this clinic to provide Walter and our other cats with the best care because they specialized in treating only cats. It made sense; at least until it didn't anymore. As we discussed this, I found myself shifting from despondent to just plain angry. It was becoming very apparent that Walter's death might have been premature. Adenocarcinoma, if detected early in a cat, can potentially be curative if removed before metastasis. I even remember the internal medicine vet telling me this during our initial phone call. Our grieving was now taking a new direction. I realized that something had been nagging me for a long time surrounding the cat clinic's role in Walter's care. It was now pretty obvious what it was.

Imagine you have an older family member (age in the seventies) who had a long history of GI issues. You take him into his primary care physician, as he has progressively lost weight and has other symptoms, such as loss of appetite, diarrhea, etc. The primary care physician examines him, draws labs, and then diagnoses him with IBD and pancreatitis. Unbeknownst to you, she notes cancer as a differential diagnosis but doesn't mention this. She also doesn't order any other diagnostics to make a truly definitive diagnosis such as endoscopy, ultrasound, CT scan, or even an abdominal X-ray. She does not suggest a referral to a GI specialist at this time but prescribes steroids, an appetite stimulant, and vitamin B12 injections. There are no dietary changes advised to assist with helping him to gain weight until you request at a later date for nutritional advisement. You reach out to communicate with the PCP several times over the next several months as the condition does not improve. No changes to the plan are given. Finally, after four months have gone by, your family member is really struggling, and you cannot accept his condition anymore. You bring him back in and his lab work is catastrophically worse on recheck, which matches his physical deterioration. The PCP sits you down and says:

"Well, he is older."

You bristle at this because he is otherwise healthy, and who would have the audacity to say this about your beloved family member anyways? Finally, the PCP says it's time for him to go see a GI specialist, and she now recommends an abdominal ultrasound.

The PCP doesn't offer abdominal ultrasounds but has a GI specialist who comes in and does them on a very limited basis that is incompatible with your work schedule. You decide to make an appointment with their GI referral specialist on your own but cannot get in for a month. Once you see the specialist, she suspects cancer, but her diagnostic work is inconclusive. She decides to put him on antibiotics in case this is not cancer and then plans to repeat all the diagnostic work in a month. When that time comes, she then informs you she will not be available for another month. You are disgusted by her lack of concern for your family member. It's now been six months since you've seen the PCP, and your family member is really struggling. You seek out alternative providers and plead with another GI specialist to squeeze your family member in urgently, but even this takes several weeks.

The clock keeps ticking as finally he is seen by the new specialist. You are desperate for answers. Thankfully, they are able to diagnosis this accurately in only three days. However, your heart stops and drops when you are informed that your family member has Adenocarcinoma of the descending colon. You now plead for a surgical consult for immediate removal of this mass, knowing it might've already spread.

You think about the six wasted months. You think about the PCP diagnosing and treating without doing the appropriate diagnostic tests. You think about the additional wasted time due to their poor referral. What kind of of PCP practice is this?

Your mind is reeling. Your frail family member is so anemic by the time surgery rolls around that they require a blood transfusion prior to surgery. Due to potential transfusion reaction, the blood transfusion itself increases his risk before, during, and after surgery. The poor patient has been left in such a compromised state that his surgical risk under anesthesia is now radically increased as well. There is a very real chance he could die before, during, or after this surgery. You bemoan how his blood count has plummeted in the last six months. Wasn't anyone paying attention? Why didn't the PCP inform you that his blood work was significantly lower at his appointment in late October? You spend the entire day of his surgery scared; every moment feels like you are on pins and needles.

Thankfully, your family member pulls through surgery. In fact, post operatively, he is doing quite well thanks to his toughness and the skill of the providers at the hospital. You are relieved and feel a sense of optimism. The optimism is unfortunately short-lived when the pathology report comes back. His cancer has extensively spread into his omentum and lymph nodes. You think about all the wasted time. What if they had appropriately caught this much earlier? You think about the six wasted months. They give your beloved family member a poor prognosis of only two months to live, as this is now considered an advanced cancer. You ignore the statistics and fight like hell to save him. Despite your best efforts, he only lives another eight months. He dies an agonizing death. You are devastated. Your family is devastated. In the back of your mind, you think about the PCP. Two words start creeping into to the forefront of your grieving brain: negligence and malpractice.

The previous clinical scenario is fictitious. Fictitious in the sense that its not about a person but rather a cat. Our cat. This is precisely the course that Walter's treatment took between July 2020 and his surgery in February 2021. We finally realized that his cancer course could have taken a different direction. It was potentially way more treatable and perhaps even curative if early detection and diagnosis were appropriately utilized. My wife and I realized that, despite his absence, Walter's legacy would have to be honored. #JusticeforWalti.

Full disclosure. I never once considered Walter's story or this book to go in this direction. I was praying I'd be writing this book for a long time to catch up on current events in Walter's tale of survival, or it would be a much shorter story designed to enlighten, encourage, and perhaps assist pet owners faced with similar scenarios. It's conflicting to think that this material or any reference made to veterinary medicine and veterinarians in a derogatory way serves any good purpose. Walter literally had a team of vets hired to assist him in his fight against cancer. In all, there were eight veterinarians of varying specialties and backgrounds that I happily shelled out many desperate dollars to in an attempt to save our beloved family member's life. Six of the eight were really good—or, in fact, great—providers, and we are thankful to have been blessed with their help. The remaining two were not good, and the reasons for this are readily laid out. My hope is that any pet owner reading this book does due diligence in choosing a vet who will be a good and competent fit in their pet's life. In Walter's case, I believe our poor choice of vet practice in the beginning started him down a path that was not consistent with his best interests. Our reasons for choosing were solid, but the decision itself I will forever regret. None of Walter's vets will be named, as that would be inappropriate.

I sent the cat clinic a certified letter return receipt requested. I needed to let let them know that we were not happy. I suspect they already knew this because I had called and let them know in no uncertain terms that their referral was awful many months back. I had not heard back from them once during Walter's ordeal until the sea wall incident occurred. The disappointing part of the message they left for me was it didn't inquire about Walter at all.

"Hi, we just received a report that you fell off your sea wall and were calling to see if you were "okay."

Gee, thanks for checking on me. And yes, our cat is still alive, you remember him, don't you? My wife was way more pissed off about this oversight than I was, but it bothered me as well. The letter was designed to be cathartic for us and to make them aware that we knew about the negligence. I did not ask for any type of refund. Anything they would even consider refunding was not going to bring Walter back. In addition, how do you request a refund from a vet who didn't do much of anything? No, we needed them to know how we felt. The letter made reference to a potential complaint report to the Board of Veterinary Medicine. We also informed that we were keeping all our options open. This had us thirsting for justice written all over it. The wheels were now turning, and options were, in fact, being considered.

My family were extremely supportive during this time period. It's times like these that you are grateful to lean on those you love the most. I was on the phone with my oldest brother, who owns many exotic birds. He is definitely able to relate about animal experiences. During this conversation, I mentioned to my brother that we were considering hiring an attorney to draft a complaint letter. At first glance, this sounds insane. At second glance, it doesn't. I described in great detail of how this missed diagnosis may have prematurely ended Walter's life. As we spoke, it became obvious to both of us that justice was a dish best served cold. The amount of pain and suffering we had experienced was real and palpable. We didn't blame anyone for his cancer. We blamed for how they missed it. It became readily apparent that speaking to an attorney would be a viable option.

I'm not sure if it was fate, but we located an attorney within two hours of where we live who is also a veterinarian. In fact, he practices within the growing field of animal law. We surely were not the first to feel that a vet had acted with negligence or malpractice. In fact, a short online search proved this to be true. We found the Animal Defense League's website. Their website was priceless; it contained much valuable information. We were glad there are organizations like them that exist to provide a voice for animals. We were attempting to provide a voice for Walter. The voice of justice. The price was hardly outrageous to arrange a consult and draft a complaint letter. #JusticeforWalti.

The process for initiating a legal consult was simple. We had to forward medical records that the attorney would review prior to the consult. If he felt we had a case, we would discuss the options. I forwarded the records for the cat clinic, referring vet, and the vet practice that completed Walter's internal medicine diagnosis, surgery and chemo. I actually wrote a six-page letter to the attorney laying out who we were and why we felt the need to pursue relief.

The case, in my eyes, was pretty simple. It was a clear case of negligence to diagnose our cat without use of appropriate diagnostic tests. I included an article from the CATMANDO blogsite, where the highly competent contributing vet discussed a case scenario almost identical to Walter's. He stressed the need and efficacy of routine abdominal ultrasound in order to make a diagnosis. Sadly, the cat clinic apparently had not read his blog.

In the days leading up to the legal consult, we received the ashes for Water's sister Simba. My wife picked them up, and it was a crushing experience for her. The day I picked up Walter's ashes in an urn was absolutely one of the saddest days of my entire life. I was crying when I walked in, and then completely fell apart on the car ride home. The outpouring of grief was profound, and the reality of permanent loss was brutal. I realized that day that my wife and I lived through a constant feeling of stress and duress for almost 14 months. It seemed we had a form of PTSD afterwards as well.

The house seemed empty without two thirds of our feline family. During the last few days, my wife and I had both heard noises in our home that sounded a lot like Walter was still with us. I had two dreams that he visited me, and my wife had a dream that he was in our bed cuddling with us. One morning, I was leaving for work and put something in my trunk. I shut the trunk and then heard what sounded like a Walter meow. I looked around, didn't see anything, and said, "Walter if that's you, I miss you and love you."

The neighbors luckily weren't around to witness this. When I got home that evening, my wife and I both heard the familiar sound of a cat jumping off the bed upstairs and landing on the floor with a thud. Problem is, we were downstairs with Mayfield, our only remaining cat. On a day off from work, I was taking a 30-minute nap. While lying in bed, I felt the familiar weight of a cat now on the bed. I even heard and felt the light movement that a cat's little paws make. Our remaining cat was downstairs. I sat up, looked around and didn't see anything. *Am I going crazy?*

No, I don't think I'm crazy; at least, not very crazy. I know what I felt. I secretly hoped it was Walter looking in on me. I have no rational explanation. In reading about these experiences, apparently, they are more common that you might think. If Walter is, in fact, visiting us from beyond, I'm sure he knows how much we miss him; you can't miss it.

The legal consult was interesting. Our attorney was both a retired vet and an attorney specializing in animal law cases. Our consult consisted of us going over the medical records, and he had questions about dates and events. He was surprised that there weren't more records from the cat specialty practice in question. He felt like the best course of action would be to send a demand letter. This letter would ask for a specific dollar amount (in our case, the cost of all visits following their negligence). I would never ask for the cost of surgery, chemo, or the vaccine, as these would've occurred regardless. I wasn't blaming this vet practice for the cancer itself, as that was unavoidable. I was seeking justice for how they ignored and misdiagnosed his cancer, which led to ultimately almost seven months of wasted time. Had this been caught early, he potentially could still be alive and well.

Rehashing all of this was mentally exhausting and sad. It opened still healing wounds and left me depressed. Still, we pushed on and began the process of formatting a letter.

When you are researching potential legal action against a vet, it's a slippery slope. The law does not typically recognize your pet as anything more than a chair. In other words, if you paid $30 for your cat, that's the damages you might expect to recover. "Property" is how they apparently classify your beloved pet. Another oddity is the malpractice companies that cover vets against potential litigation. According to our attorney, oftentimes the malpractice company will be willing to fight and spend more money defending their client that what the proposed settlement amount is. I suppose the malpractice companies do not want to set a legal precedent by settling cases, which could motivate more people to hold vets accountable when they make mistakes. When you put all these factors together, it becomes readily apparent that it's a daunting challenge to challenge a vet practice in the legal system.

That being the case, we were undaunted. Walter was not our personal property, a chair, or an inanimate object. He was a beautiful and loving, living being and deserved to be treated as such. He was family.

As we embarked on what we perceived to be justice for our beloved cat, we had some mixed feelings about the route we were taking. We certainly did not have a vendetta against or any preconceived negative notions about veterinarians. Our experiences with veterinarians were a mixed bag. Most of them were very good and conveyed genuine caring. Some of the practices, however, did not measure up to others. There does seem to exist a widespread in competency levels amongst vet practices. The overall take home message is that, unfortunately, it falls on the owners to be the voice and advocate for their pets. Sadly, this involves being willing and able to make sure your chosen veterinarian is fully vetted. Prior to enrolling our cats as patients, we looked at reviews at the cat specialty practice in question, but they were all very positive. One red flag should've been them calling themselves a "cat hospital." In retrospect, this was very misleading, as they did not offer surgery; they did not offer ultrasound services; they never volunteered any type of radiologic services; etc. Having an intimate knowledge of what hospitals are and aren't, this should have raised a red flag, but prior to Walter's experience, we did not know. I'm writing this book in the hopes that it helps pet owners take better care of their beloved furry family members. Truly taking the best care of them means being educated about their current and potential health issues and being involved in their care.

Another issue with pursuing accountability for Walter's poor veterinary care was the scab it was pulling off. We were, and might forever be, grieving his death. When you are peeling back the layers of the onion to see what went wrong, you are peeling off the scabs of grieving. My wife and I cried a lot as we went back over his medical records, reliving the pain and agony of Walter's pain and agony. In the back of my mind, I had to keep reminding myself that this was to grant justice and closure for Walter. I also was intent on helping another potential pet owner attempt to avoid what we all went through if possible.

I spent a lot of time providing our attorney with a treasure trove of information relating to the time frame, events, and what we perceived to be blatant malpractice by the veterinarian in question. In another way, it was cathartic to think that perhaps holding this veterinarian responsible for her actions might prevent someone else from going through what we did. I felt like I probably put in way more time in helping to craft this demand letter than the lawyer did himself. I was fine with that if it meant justice might be served. The letter itself asked for a settlement. It also mentioned that we would consider filing a report to the Board of Veterinary Medicine and potentially involving our right to express our feelings on social media. The money meant very little to us, as it was not a lot and would make no difference in our lives. The order of the day was justice for Walter. There was no amount of money that could bring him back or allow us to go back in time to change the course of events.

Several weeks passed without receiving an update. Finally, our attorney reached out to let us know they had rejected our settlement offer. The reasoning behind this was that according to the malpractice company's representative, "The vet had offered us all diagnostics and we declined." Nothing could be further from the truth. In fact, the vet's own notes stated, "Owner states interested in all diagnostics and wants him to live a long time." What a stark contrast from "owners declined all diagnostics." This was cover your ass to infinity and beyond. My wife and I were now very determined to file the complaint letter to the board of vet medicine as well and immediately started the draft. The scab that had been left open had now grown larger. As in death and in life, we were fighting for Walter. This time, it was to receive a taste of justice for his premature departure from his loving family and this world.

The attorney also immediately sent a rebuttal letter, which laid out, incredulously, just how false these statements were. In addition, in these cases, the medical records do not lie. The statements provided to our attorney were simply not supported by the medical records that we were in possession of.

It dawned on me that perhaps the vet had falsified the records. The attorney's letter mentioned this and reminded the lying side of how serious this would be. We were angry but knew this would be a time-consuming process, and there would be no quick resolution. My wife and I began the process in earnest of going over the medical records again, and I started writing the complaint letter to the Board of Veterinary Medicine. In the back of my mind, I was determined to not let this vet do this to anyone else's beloved cat, dog, or any other type of animal. It was too late to save Walter, but what if we could prevent this from happening to someone else? Armed with all of the relevant information, it was not difficult to quickly put together a formal complaint.

Pursuant to the attorney's complaint, the correspondence to the Vet Board contained the same material. The focus was on the vet's failure to recognize potential cancer signs, failure to suggest diagnostic tests based on the obvious signs of potential cancer as a diagnosis, blindly treating for IBD without utilizing adequate tests to rule out cancer, failure of the vet to adjust or change the plan for four months while Walter continued to deteriorate, and now the utter and complete dishonestly with attempting to blame us while contradicting the medical records. I attached all relevant medical records along with about four pages of explanation concerning dates, events, and medical information. Our goal at the very least would be for the vet in question to adjust her practice moving forward in order to prevent this from happening to someone else's pet. It was now crystal clear to us that there must exist a very large spread of competency in veterinary medicine. Much like normal human healthcare, there are good providers and poor providers, sometimes even in the same practice. Unfortunately, we came across a poor one, and she was dishonest as well. The scabs of our experience were open, and we frequently relived the pain. To say we had some slight PTSD from this was perhaps an understatement. See below the letter that we sent to the Vet Board.

*****

*****

*****

*****

David I Antokal

*****

****

*Dear *****,*

*I am presenting this complaint based on our experience with ***** more specifically *****. A little background information on myself. My wife and I relocated to ***** in 2019. I have consulted with and retained ***** for this matter.*

The fundamental question that needs to be answered here is:

Can a veterinarian make a diagnosis and blindly treat without utilizing or at least offering appropriate diagnostic tests? *Is it a breach of veterinary standards of practice and care if they do? In relation to human medicine, I can assure you that this would be negligence/malpractice every time guaranteed with both disciplinary action and likely litigation to follow by injured or deceased parties. I present a simple analogy. Could you imagine going to your doctor with a medical issue and having your doctor diagnose and treat you without using any appropriate diagnostic tests that are readily available. What if your doctor diagnosed you with colitis without ordering an ultrasound, abdominal X-ray, CT, endoscopy, etc. Imagine how you'd feel 6 months later receiving a terminal cancer diagnosis that might've been more treatable if only your doctor had ordered the appropriate diagnostic tests.* **This is exactly how ***** treated and failed our beloved and now deceased cat Walter.**

Our cat Walter was under the care of ***** from May 30, 2019 to October 30, 2020. We chose this practice based on their advertising of being a "full service cat hospital" that specializes in cats. Based on their advertising, we put our trust in this practice to ensure Walter received the best possible care. Walter had a long history of chronic constipation which had been previously treated with multiple deobstipation procedures, lactulose, cisapride, and dietary changes. ***** were given all of Walter's previous medical records and in May 2019 they noted weight loss. At his repeat exam on July 2020, ***** noted a further decrease in weight. She also noted in the records that "Owner wants him to live a long time and is interested in diagnostics".

As the medical records show, ***** included "neoplasia" as a differential diagnosis. Despite this, ***** only ordered bloodwork (see medical record from July 2020). There were no recommendations for an ultrasound, imaging, biopsies (endoscopy), or any other action taken to rule out neoplasia vs. IBD. ***** ***blindly diagnosed and treated Walter for IBD with no diagnostic work to back up this diagnosis.*** *As we all know, blood work cannot differentiate between IBD and neoplasia (either lymphoma or adenocarcinoma).*

I have attached all relevant medical records for your review. ***Medical records do not lie****. ***** need to explain to a committee of their peers how this was an acceptable treatment plan for our cat. Why was it OK to diagnose* and treat blindly especially when they had documented possible neoplasia as a differential diagnosis in the medical records? If you cared enough to document "the owner is interested in diagnostics", why didn't you order or refer?

In any branch of human medicine, this case would be an open and shut case of blatant medical negligence. Diagnosing without appropriate diagnostic work would be so far below the threshold for meeting any reasonable standard of care and practice and would be indefensible in a deposition. I understand that Veterinarians are held to a standard of care and practice. **Does the standard of care and practice include performing or at least recommending diagnostic work to support a diagnosis?**

Sadly in this case, we were sent home with an IBD diagnosis. Prednisone, appetite stimulant, and vitamin B12 were prescribed and I later called in to request a dietary plan to hopefully assist with Walter's continued weight loss. Over the course of the next 4 months, Walter's condition continued to deteriorate. His appetite was poor, his weight loss continued, and his energy level dropped. We received no further recommendations from *****. Finally in October, we returned to ***** as it was apparent Walter's medical status was continuing to deteriorate despite our best efforts (see medical records). We followed up many times but no change to treatment plan was provided by ***** This obviously was a time sensitive period but went unrecognized by ***** The wasted time due to their negligence is a critical element to the tragedy that followed.

At the return visit, they repeated labs (suggested possible pancreatitis) and I sat down in the lobby with *****. She informed me that at this time, it was best that Walter saw an internal medicine vet. When I inquired further she stated "You know, he is about 80 in human years". I found this statement to be mortifying. My mother is 86, should we give up and hoist the white flag if she falls ill because she is elderly? Wow. ***** informed me that they did not offer ultrasound but did have a vet who occasionally performed them at her office. The scheduling was not a fit with either mine or my wife's schedule so we sought to see her consulting vet (*****) at her own practice (*****). Unbeknownst to us, Walter's lab work showed a dramatic turn for the worse. He was now very anemic and his labs indicated a pronounced inflammatory process very consistent with neoplasia. In retrospect, I find it deeply disturbing

that ***** did not share these lab results with us. In fact, until I requested Walter's medical records, I was completely unaware of the dramatic change in his labs from July to October. Of note, ***** notes state Walter had a history of "megacolon". We provided ***** with all of Walter's previous medical records. He was never diagnosed with megacolon. Was ***** paying attention or was she just going through the motions?

At this point, we were going on 5 months from the July 2020 visit. Why is this relevant?

The IBD that ***** blindly diagnosed Walter with was found to be adeno-carcinoma of the large colon. **Had ***** taken the reasonable action of ordering appropriate diagnostic work or at least referring us to someone who could in July, Walter's cancer would've been caught much earlier. In fact, it's possible his cancer might've been caught prior to metastasis which could've dramatically extended his life.**

As it was, the referring internal medicine vet ***** performed an ultrasound guided biopsy which proved inconclusive. She then elected to treat with antibiotics (in case it was a granulomatous process) and wanted to repeat diagnostics in one month. We were now at 6 months with no diagnosis. In January, we decided to take Walter to ***** and received a diagnosis within 3 days. It was adenocarcinoma. Walter went into surgery in early February (now a full 7 months since the July 2020 appointment at *****). He was so anemic that he required a blood transfusion prior to surgery. Walter survived surgery and was given a very grave prognosis due to the adenocarcinoma metastasizing into the lymph nodes and omentum. Despite the grave prognosis, we threw everything we could at his cancer. We hired a holistic veterinarian, hired an oncologist at ***** for chemo, got him the Torigen autologous cancer vaccine, and finally attempted Immunocidin after the cancer recurred elsewhere in his abdomen. We were desperate and failing at trying to save our beloved cat. It was blood, sweat, and many tears. This post surgical treatment also cost in excess of $8,000.

Walter's last abdominal ultrasound was done in August, one month prior to his tragic death.

That ultrasound, performed at ***** showed that Walter had a tumor that had gotten larger attached to his abdominal wall, and additional tumors in his omentum. A chest X-ray now showed metastasis into his lungs. **Amazingly,**

79

Walter had no recurrence of the cancer in his colon. So if ***** had followed the standard of care/practice and suggested appropriate diagnostic work in early July 2020, would Walter's cancer have potentially been curative with a colectomy with reanastomosis? According to *****, certainly a possibility in some cases. What is a wasted 7 months in human years? It is said that cats over the age of 2 age about 4 times as fast as humans. Could you imagine one of your family members having 28 months wasted while a cancer grew inside of them that was missed by their doctor? You would certainly want the doctor to be held accountable wouldn't you? My wife and I will forever be sick about this. We don't blame ***** for Walter's cancer. We blame them for lazy veterinary care and negligence. If Walter's cancer had been caught in a timely fashion back in July, he would've had a fighting chance. Review the medical records that I've attached. Would you want to have ***** treating one of your furry family members? Had I known then what I know now, I wouldn't either.

I also would like to point out something about ***** role at the Cat clinic ***** is apparently very active with online veterinary blogs. She apparently veered more into euthanasia and hospice practice about 10 years ago. She seems to post a lot about how she didn't enjoy regular veterinary practice and much prefers her new career tract. If this is the case, why did ***** feel it appropriate to be taking care of high acuity patients at a cat specialty clinic where they advertise on their website "how critical early diagnosis and treatment is". The website for ***** states "The American Veterinary Medical Association now recommends having semiannual exams on all cats regardless of lifestyle. A single year in a cat's life is significant. Physical changes and medical conditions occur more rapidly with age. Cats are masters at hiding disease and there are a number of medical problems for which early detection can literally be a lifesaver. Through frequent routine examinations and yearly wellness testing the doctor can gather a wealth of information concerning the well being of your cat(s)". ***** apparently didn't get the memo regarding "early detection". See attached "Catmando" blog about how a good veterinarian who follows standards of care and practice treats patients similar to Walter's case and then compare that to the sub standard care Walter received at *****.

On September 30, 2021 Walter died in my arms gasping for air one hour before his in home euthanasia appointment. It was heartbreaking to lose our beloved family member. Despite our best efforts and over $15,000 spent on medical treatment, we felt like we failed him as he took his last breath. After his death, we had time to reflect on his long battle with cancer. The overwhelming thought process goes back to the critical wasted time between July and February. That cascade of wasted time falls directly on *****'s negligence.

I would like to be kept informed about the actions taken by the board in relation to this complaint. My attorney and I are keeping all options open. I decided to handle this complaint on my own in order to conserve funds. I would like to see this vet be held accountable and disciplined for the substandard care and obvious breach of veterinary standards of care and practice. My legacy gift to Walter's memory is trying to prevent this from happening to someone else's beloved cat. That is worth more to us than any financial settlement we might receive. Irregardless, we will never get our beloved cat back and he needlessly suffered more than he should have due to their negligence.

Sincerely,

David I Antokal

Several months went by with nary an update. Then, the first update arrived. The malpractice rep for the vet in question responded to our attorney with a bizarre request. She requested all of the information she had already received as if the process had just started. This was sadly not unexpected, as it appeared to be further stonewalling. The attorney sent a rather curt reply to the effect of, "You've had this information for months, why are you requesting it again"? We were pretty convinced this was not going to go anywhere at this point. However, we knew that the vet in question was now being shelled from both directions and that she would have to answer for her negligence. Win, lose, or draw, we had voiced our disgust and at least the process for a semblance of justice was moving forward. In fact, the next response was affirming. The vet board responded with an update informing us that the attorneys had found "probable cause" to send this complaint forward to a vet

committee. We shared the update with the attorney and felt rather hopeful that they would at least take a very hard look at the case.

A few months passed, and we heard back from the vet board via snail mail. The gist was that they carefully reviewed the file but found insufficient evidence to support any disciplinary action against the vet in question. I was not surprised by this but disappointed by the result. I had mixed feelings as well. On the one hand, we wanted the vet to be held accountable. On the other hand, we didn't want to destroy someone's capacity to earn a living. Somewhere in between, we also didn't want this to happen to someone else's beloved cat or dog. My wife was livid, and yet more tears were shed by both of us. You see, every time we got immersed in this process, it pulled the scab off a little more and brought back such sad memories.

We had reached the end of the road, it seemed, in relation to the legal and administrative accountability aspects of Walter's death. To date, we have not heard back from the attorney, so the assumption is that the case has sailed its course. While disappointing, we feel that we made our feelings known, and perhaps, this was a needed learning experience for the vet involved. As it pertained to the vet board, we likewise felt like they were supplied with a lot of overwhelming evidence and yet either couldn't or wouldn't act on it. Perhaps it was a "good old boys' network," where the board wouldn't incriminate one of its own. The politics involved in a case like this in any discipline would always certainly be present and is just the reality of day to day human life. It is also possible that they felt like there was some cause but not enough to proceed forward. The truly disturbing part of this whole process was the blame game shifting by the vet and her malpractice company. Blaming the client instead of accepting some responsibility for her actions was truly devious and dishonest, in our opinion. This aspect was perhaps the most disturbing piece of this sad and twisted puzzle.

While both roads to justice failed to intersect, our mourning for Walter continued. It could be a sad song on the radio, a commercial of a tuxedo cat on television, or reminiscing about how awesome he was. The tears readily flowed when our thoughts gravitated to our beloved and beautiful cat who was now resting in heaven. I feel that perhaps our thoughts and dreams of

the departed are a form of reminder from them to let you know they are think-ing of you. I frequently would pick up the box of Walter's ashes and kiss them, speaking softly to him and letting him know I loved and missed him so much. It's amazing what a profound piece of your life a fur baby can become. I will forever be grateful for the time I shared with Walter and pray that I will see him again in the afterlife.

Now, almost a year after Walter's tragic death, it's both sad and introspec-tive looking back at the events. If I could turn back the clock, I would've ob-viously yanked him out of the cat specialist clinic early on and sought a second opinion sooner. I feel strongly it would've extended his life. I also wonder if it was right to have bombarded Walter with all of the treatments, both tradi-tional, alternative, and experimental. I rationalize to myself that I committed to fight for him no matter what until the end. Did we take this too far? Did he suffer needlessly undergoing treatments instead of living out his days let-ting nature take its course? I suppose it's fruitless to ruminate, as it won't change anything. There are no do-overs in this life. There is no dress rehearsal. One thing I do know for certain is that I loved Walter so much and wish he was still with us. I have to make peace with knowing I did the best I could for him both in life and in death.

I would encourage everyone reading this to love and cherish every moment you have with your fur babies. I felt every day I spent with Walter was like opening a special gift on Christmas morn-ing. I really cherished every mo-ment and wished they lasted forever. It seems like life is a col-lection of fleeting moments. I suppose the goal is to relish the great moments and minimize the bad ones.

Be an advocate for your pets. Research and be up to date on issues related to their health. Know that they need a voice, your voice, to ensure they receive the best care possible. Research your veterinary practice and make sure you know who will be taking care of your loved ones. Make sure to meet all the vets and make sure you are comfortable with all of them. There is absolutely a wide range of clinical competency in veterinary care, so do your homework. Above all, when they really need you, get ready to stand up and fight for them. Be #WalterStrong.

Rest in peace Walter. We love you.